MUSICAL INVOLVEMENT

A GUIDE TO PERCEPTIVE LISTENING

==================== SECOND EDITION ====================

DONALD J. FUNES
California State University, San Marcos

With the assistance of
STEPHEN E. SQUIRES
Northern Illinois University

HARCOURT BRACE JOVANOVICH COLLEGE PUBLISHERS

Fort Worth   Philadelphia   San Diego   New York   Orlando   Austin   San Antonio
Toronto   Montreal   London   Sydney   Tokyo

Acquisitions Editor: Cynthia L. Kumagawa, Julia Berrisford
Manuscript Editor: Natalie Bowen
Production Editor: Judi McClellan
Designer: Cathy Reynolds
Art Editor: Louise Sandy-Karkoutli
Production Manager: Lynne Bush

COVER CREDIT: *Oda a la Alegria* by Graciela Rodo Boulanger. Courtesy of Lublin Graphics, Inc., Greenwich, CT.

ISBN: 0-15-564952-3

Library of Congress Catalog Card Number: 90-81892

Printed in the United States of America

To Carolyn Funes for her love, confidence, and encouragement.

PREFACE

This brief introduction to music, designed for quarter or semester courses, presupposes no musical training of any kind. The only prerequisite for its use is the willingness to become an activist in listening to music and in creating musical experiences, with students and instructor together pursuing the goal of musical perceptiveness through musical involvement.

The book does not divide music into categories—"good" or "bad," "popular" or "classical," "ours" or "theirs"—and it does not describe traditional styles or retell music history. What the book does do is reach out toward the music of all cultures and times, taking in music of Africa and Asia along with Western folk music, rock, jazz, the standard concert repertory, and the frontiers of composition today. All these are explored for the features they share: sound, time, rhythm, pitch, and the orderly effects of growth and structure. Running through the step-by-step focus on each of these elements is the unifying concept of tension-and-repose cycles. In comment and example, each element is probed in terms of these ever-recurring cycles that are central to whatever impact music makes on us.

Throughout the book, two principal devices frame the students' activist role:

1. Questions to be answered. Concentrated listening is required to answer these direct questions about a specific musical event at a given moment in a particular piece. The answers—often simple and always brief—are supplied in an Instructor's Manual.
2. Independent projects. A variety of individual and group projects invite creative participation in composing and performing at whatever level each student can command. All the projects reinforce some particular concept, and all are designed to enhance listening by doing.

In addition, many of the photographs encourage students to reach beyond music in an active exploration of parallels in the other arts. By all these means, this book and its numerous recorded musical illustrations aim to aid the development of that full involvement that alone provides the ultimate rewards of listening.

The second edition of *Musical Involvement* maintains the same pedagogical thinking as the original version. A full one-third of the material is new. Chapter One, "Our Sound Environment" has been completely recast to reflect current practices in ethnomusicology. Chapter Two is a new chapter devoted to understanding and perceiving the human voice. In addition, the topic of tonality is covered with completely new materials. The distinctly different approaches to tonality are clearly explained and explored. Finally, every question in the book has been evaluated for relevance and accuracy.

The stance and substance of this book come out of the crucible of the 1960s. In particular personal ways, they were affected by Robert Trotter of the University of Oregon and by Jane M. Saunders. In broader terms they were shaped by the musical life and times of our students and by the seminal ideas of John Cage, Leonard Meyer, and Marshall McLuhan. I owe a great deal to the vision and faith of Nina Gunzenhauser and Julia Berrisford and must acknowledge a special debt to my editor, Natalie Bowen, whose sure hand and sharp editorial skills guided the later stages of both the first and second editions. I would also like to thank, the staff of Harcourt Brace Jovanovich who worked on this edition: Cynthia L. Kumagawa, acquisitions editor; Judi McClellan, production editor; Louise Sandy-Karkoutli, art editor; Cathy Reynolds, designer; and Lynne Bush, production manager.

I owe a special debt of thanks to a group of talented colleagues that recorded a number of musical examples for this book and who shared their musical and technical insights with me. The list includes Cynthia and Gene Dybdahl, Steve Gorn, Robert Chappell, Robert Reeves, John Fairfield, Debu Prasad Banerjee, Han Kuo-Huang, William Koehler and especially Peter Middleton. I would also like to acknowledge the following individuals for their valuable contributions: Elizabeth Wehrman, Western Illinois University; Joseph L. Casey, DePaul University School of Music; Stephen Glover, Butler University; Elyse Mach, Northeastern Illinois University; Brent Heisinger, San Jose State University; and Howard Hudiburg, Jr., Southwest Texas State University. Finally, my sincere thanks to Stephen Squires and Gayle Rosenwinkel who made the preparation of the second edition possible.

Donald J. Funes

CONTENTS

INTRODUCTION

Hearing music and responding to it actively is *listening,* something very different from merely basking in agreeable sounds. This book will help you learn to listen—to heighten your musical awareness, develop a number of listening skills, and involve yourself in music, old and new, music of the Americas, Africa, Asia, and Europe.

It would certainly be understandable for you to be somewhat skeptical if you were told that there are a number of different ways of listening. For most people the act requires no special effort. We are surrounded by sounds—there is no complete silence in everyday life. Whether it is the mechanical noises within a building, music playing in the background, street sounds, muffled voices from another room, the sound of tree branches being moved by the wind, or the sound of your own breathing, there is no shortage of auditory stimulation. Ironically, in situations that often require a very quiet environment

A group of young people listen to live music.

such as a concert, a lecture, the library, or a play, the little sounds that are always a part of our environment suddenly become intrusive. While the sound of a candy wrapper or feet moving under a chair, the hum of fluorescent lights or very soft talking are only marginally perceivable in everyday life, they can become very obvious when we are in a state of high auditory focus (that is, when we are attending carefully to a specific sound source other than these peripheral sounds).

Psychologists tell us that we can attend to around seven sensory inputs simultaneously. If this is true, the mind can get cluttered with extraneous auditory information at times when a single focus is appropriate. Luckily, we can learn to restrict our attention to a small number of auditory signals. This type of listening is not automatic.

The task of careful listening is further complicated by other sources. You have all carried on internal monologues or dialogues in silence. At this precise moment while you are reading, you may be having such a separate internal conversation. The conversation may or may not have anything to do with the material on this page. You may be saying the words you are reading or reflecting on the ideas while you read, or you may be rehearsing a conversation you plan to have with your professor or with a friend. This irrelevant activity has to be counted as one of the seven inputs. If you have ever had to read a paragraph over and over because your internal dialogue and other real sounds drew your attention away from the meaning of the words, you will understand the point of this discussion. Listening to music requires listeners to minimize the distracting (internal or external) influences outside of the actual music so they can notice important details of the work being presented. This is not an easy task but it is an extremely rewarding way to interact with music.

It is, however, not the only way to interact with music. Music can be a powerful agent for relaxation. Many people enjoy studying or socializing while music is in the background. It is hard to imagine a dramatic film without a supporting musical score; everyone experiences music in this manner. The type of listening skills you will develop here relies on most of your positive former experiences with music of all kinds in all contexts. You will doubtless continue to have many meaningful experiences in life that involve music.

The materials and exercises in *Musical Involvement* will focus your listening attention in a very specific way. You will learn to listen to music as an aesthetic object. In order to hear music this way you must adopt an aesthetic attitude. It's a crucial but easy step in the progression toward perceptive listening.

THE AESTHETIC ATTITUDE

Whether consciously or not, your perceptions of and your responses to experiences, people, and objects are guided by a set of preconditioned responses. For example, if you are angry at a friend everything your friend does bothers you. Simple things like the pronunciation of certain words or a hand gesture become additional reasons for you to be angry. If your attitude were different—more positive in this case—you might not even notice the little things that are driving you crazy.

A common example of the influence one's attitude can have on perception is the eight-ounce glass containing four ounces of water. How would you describe the glass? Is it half full or half empty? If you can think of it both ways, you will know how easy it is to change your attitude about an experience.

But what is an aesthetic attitude? Aesthetics is the branch of philosophy that concerns itself with theories of beauty and the arts. In this sense the word "aesthetic" refers to the perception of beauty embodied in musical compositions. But you don't need to develop a special theory of beauty and art to adopt an aesthetic attitude; you simply need to decide that it is a potentially useful way to interact with sound. Your attitude will guide you.

Now the tricky part. Many aestheticians (specialists in the field of aesthetics) state that in order to experience a piece of music aesthetically you must *distance* yourself from it. This sounds like a contradiction. Distance in this context means that all other vivid associations or thoughts that you might have about a piece of music must be set aside—deemphasized and filtered out—if you are going to perceive the music as an aesthetic object. To the degree that your mind is making pictures, or wondering about the age of the composer, the price of the concert ticket, the name of the trumpet player, or whether your professor will include the piece on a test, you are not enjoying the work aesthetically. The goal is to minimize all thoughts that vie for attention. To the degree that you can do this, you are perceiving aesthetically: you are perceiving an object, an experience, or a work of art for its own sake.

The impractical eye can find beauty anywhere—in the middle of a city street, for example, or in the swirling pipes of an oil refinery (opposite).

As an example of distancing, think of a peaceful country scene—a meadow with cattle grazing beside a stream, a stand of pine trees nearby. To a real estate developer the scene might represent six acres ripe for subdivision and profit. A scientist might see there the raw materials for ecological or geological data. A passing driver might be looking for the stream as a landmark in a set of directions. A fisherman's eyes might light up at the possibility of trout for lunch, while the farmer-owner would probably be thinking in economic terms—the health of the cattle, the condition of the alfalfa, the lumber potential of the trees. These perceptions differ, but they are all *practical:* the scene is taken in not for what it is, but as a means to some end. Though all these people might be partly free from ulterior motives, the best chance for aesthetic perception might be that of a hiker, who has no purpose other than to see, hear, smell, and enjoy. His or her experience is utterly *impractical,* an end in itself.

Walk slowly to class and try to *notice*. Listen, look, and touch.

Try to fit each of the following objects or situations into one of these five categories: biological, intellectual, moral-religious, economic, and aesthetic. You may find that some will fit into more than one category, depending on your attitude.

a bird call
a foot race
hand lotion
an advertisement showing a beautiful girl in a bikini
a line of people in a bank
a test tube

Besides distancing, another condition necessary for aesthetic perception is *sympathetic awareness,* which means an openness on your part—a willingness to set aside any prejudices, so that you do not reject a piece of music before you have confronted it fully. It means that you will enter into any musical experience on its own terms, seeking out its individuality rather than expecting what it does not promise. To reject a symphony because it is different from a pop song—or vice versa—is as counterproductive as asking for a skirt on Botticelli's Venus.

When you accept these conditions for pursuing the full possibilities of musical experience, you will inevitably refine your perception. Without any help, you would doubtless do this intuitively with much listening over a long period. But with the assistance of this book, you should be able to speed up the process, because the book will help you organize what your ear takes in so that you will notice relationships you might otherwise miss. It may also help you increase your awareness of relationships in the other arts, for in the long run, the attitudes and the modes of perception you develop in listening to music will be useful to you in confronting *all* aesthetic experiences.

THE VAST WORLD OF MUSIC

The recorded selections that accompany this book reflect the rich diversity of music. No one musical style is presented as being superior

Have you any difficulty in confronting this painting fully? Can you summon enough sympathetic awareness to try to discern and appreciate the artist's purpose? (*Woman I*, 1950–52, by Willem de Kooning. Collection, The Museum of Modern Art, New York.)

Listen to three different pieces contained on the recorded selections that accompany this book. Select the pieces by a random process. You need not even know the names of the examples. Note the example number and list the most memorable characteristic of each example in positive terms. List at least ten similarities shared by all three works.

to others. There is no single musical language—there are many. Each language has its own standard of excellence. Every musical style has generated works worthy of our attention. To become an expert in one musical style to the degree that we can perceive relevant musical details, understand a work within a social/historical context, and make meaningful evaluative judgments is a life's work.

The goal here is more general. In whatever music you listen to, try to find similarities with past listening experiences. Resist the urge you may have to make value judgments. Every time you listen aesthetically you will have a positive experience.

OUR
SOUND
ENVIRONMENT
The Instruments

Which is more musical:

- the sound of breaking glass or the sound of a violin?
- the sound of a siren or the sound of an oboe?
- the "sound" of silence or the sound of a C chord?

What is Music?

Twenty-five years ago the answers to these questions would have seemed self-evident to nearly everyone. Not today. Television and modern technology have engulfed music in a sound explosion—sounds from every culture, sounds from within the earth, sounds from the ocean floor, sounds from outer space. When the world was larger— "largeness" being a factor of the time it took to transmit information, ideas, music, and so forth—communities were relatively isolated. In an environment of isolation distinctive musical instruments and musical styles developed. Even in Western Europe, a relatively small geographical area, we find historical evidence of numerous musical cultures scattered throughout the region. Instruments and the sound of singing voices were as different as the languages. Within the borders of what we now consider sovereign countries there were wide differences in the function and content of music.

How musical instruments and musical styles spread geographically is a fascinating study. The history of musical migration, in the old, large world, was inextricably linked to the development and spread of religion, political conflicts, trade, and countless other influences.

With the dawning of rapid communications and transportation, the world became a smaller planet. The peoples of the world are now linked together. The twentieth century has witnessed the invention of the airplane, radio, television, phonograph, tape recorder, and computer. We can travel most anywhere in the world within a day. We can now hear music from all regions of the world as it is being played. Independent musical traditions continue to flourish, thankfully, but there are very few places that remain untouched by outside influences. There has never been a larger number of musical choices. Songs of protest composed in Bolivia are sung in Paris. Symphonic works composed in eighteenth-century Germany are played in Singapore. The chants of Tibetan monks are sung in California. Rock groups from American perform in China. The ubiquitous cassette player has become a standard item of apparel in many cultures, and the number of musical instruments in everyday use is bewilderingly large.

CLASSIFYING THE INSTRUMENTS

Because there are so many musical instruments in the world, a system of classification can be very complicated. The traditional Euro-American system divides instruments into the following groups: woodwind, brass, percussion, keyboard, and string. This system is useful when referring to Euro-American orchestral music but it does not accommodate instruments from other cultures and traditions.

Early in the 20th century Erich M. Hornbostel and Curt Sachs developed a classification of musical instruments based on the physics of sound production. They identified four major classes (a fifth was

A traditional Western orchestra.

added later). Each major group of instruments shares a common method of setting air into motion. Sound is produced by the rapidly moving, or vibrating, air.

The Hornbostel-Sachs classification system contains the following groups:

1. Aerophones. Flowing air (in most cases) is the primary source of vibration. This class includes all of the woodwind and brass

These Indian musicians display their instruments.

instruments from the Euro-American orchestra, the pipe organ, and hundreds of other instruments.

2. Idiophones. "Idio" indicates individuality. In other words, the actual material of the instrument vibrates and creates the sound. A few examples of idiophones are bells, gongs, and cymbals.

3. Membranophone. A tightly stretched, thin, flexible sheet of natural or synthetic material (a membrane) vibrates and creates pressure waves that become sound. Most drums are membranophones.

4. Chordophones. "Chord" in this context is a synonym for cord—a string or small rope that is stretched between fixed points. The vibrating cord creates the sound. Guitars, pianos, and violins are chordophones. The method of moving the string is of secondary importance.

5. Electrophones (added later). Electronic circuitry creates a periodic fluctuation of current that in turn generates sound-pressure waves via a loudspeaker system. The electronic components make no sounds. They control the oscillations of a loudspeaker. Synthesizers and electronic keyboards are two of the more familiar electrophones.

The actual sounds produced by musical instruments are very appealing and you do not have to know how something works to enjoy it. This discussion will simply enhance your understanding of the way instrumental sounds are produced.

All sound is created through the motion of air. If you wave your hand rapidly up and down, you can even feel the air moving but there is no detectable sound. The reason is that you have created a sufficiently strong pressure wave, but you are moving your hand too slowly. You would have to wave your hand twenty times a second to produce a perceivable pitch. We will examine the specific methods of creating sound waves of each of the five instrument groups.

AEROPHONES

At first consideration it might seem confusing to state that air is the vibrating agent in aerophones. After all, all sounds are created by vibrating air. All aerophones use a stream of air to cause the instrument to sound. While in most cases the air is supplied by the

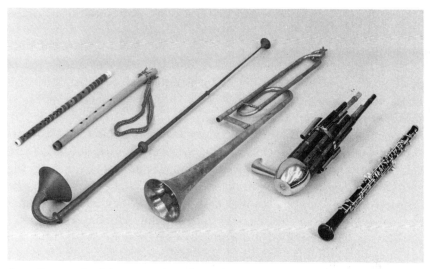

A small example of the many types of aerophones.

player, in other instruments, such as the pipe organ, the air supplied is created through mechanical means.

There are far too many aerophones in the world to describe each instrument, so we will explore just three types: flutes, reeds, and trumpets.

Flutes

The variety of flutes is vast. They range from toy whistles to symphonic silver flutes costing thousands of dollars. What all flutes have in common is that air is the primary source of vibration; the flutist's airstream is placed into motion by being directed toward a fixed, relatively sharp edge.

Anyone who has produced a sound by blowing over the open end of a bottle will recognize this principle. Obviously, not all of the air goes into the bottle all of the time. What happens is that the airstream changes its direction as it is blown against the edge, first sending more air into the bottle, then less. This alternation is the source of sound. The airstream itself is made to vibrate. In all flutes, the only minor variable to this principle is distance the air travels before it strikes the edge. On many flutes the performer blows directly against the edge (like the bottle), whereas with others the flutist's air is directed through a passageway, at the top of the instrument, until it strikes the edges, as with a whistle. Once the air strikes the edge the vibration of the airstream is the same in both types of flutes.

The accompanying photographs show a variety of flutes. All of those at the top allow the flutist to blow directly against the edge. Those at the bottom have air directed through a chamber before it strikes the edge.

To change the pitch of the first three instruments in each class, the player changes the number of holes covered or uncovered. The more holes covered, the lower the pitch. In the case of the silver flute, the performer depresses keys to cover holes. With the pan flute, like the pipe organ, each pipe plays a single pitch. With the slide whistle, the performer changes pitches by moving the plunger-like slide inside the tube. The farther the slide is inserted the shorter the tube (and the higher the pitch).

Listening Exercises

Throughout this book you will be asked to listen to musical examples. The examples are designed to help you practice your developing listening skills. Listen to every example several times with great care. You are not expected to be able to hear all you are asked to hear in one listening. If you are patient and listen to each example as many times as necessary for you to understand the points being made, you will make rapid progress toward becoming a perceptive listener.

Several multiple-choice questions appear with many of the listening examples. The examples are designed in such a way that you *should* need several repetitions of each example to guide you to a correct response.

Examples 1.1 and 1.2 feature two flutes similar in structure with distinctly different sounds. The first is for two recorders (also called the *Blockflöte* or *flauto dolce*). The recorder was very popular in Western Europe during the sixteenth, seventeenth, and eighteenth centuries. It is also popular today and is taught in some grade schools in America

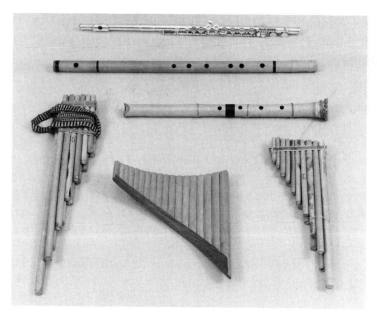

The flutist blows directly against the edge.

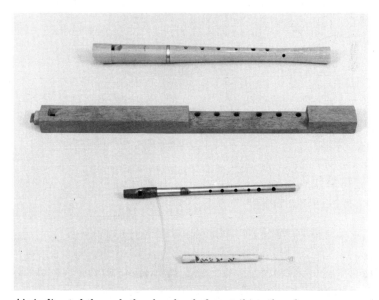

Air is directed through the chamber before striking the edge.

and Europe. In Example 1.2 the principal instrument is the tarka, a wooden flute that was developed by the indigenous people who lived in the Andes mountains of South America well before the formation of the Inca Empire.

Example 1.1   Johann Sebastian Bach *Chamber orch.*
Brandenburg Concerto No. 4, first movement (excerpt) 18th-century German composer

Two recorders are heard in this example. They are accompanied by string instruments and a harpsichord (chordophones). The example begins with one recorder sustaining a single pitch while the other plays a generally descending melody. You will recognize these short statements by the fact that each has six short chords (a combination of pitches) distributed throughout the section. You can count them easily. Two short statements are followed by a longer statement. When the long statement is concluded the two short statements return. Again each statement is supported by six chords. They are in turn followed by a longer statement. The example concludes with the return of the two short statements:

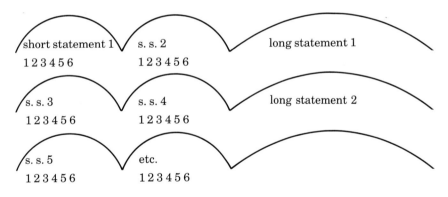

short statement 1   s. s. 2   long statement 1
1 2 3 4 5 6   1 2 3 4 5 6

s. s. 3   s. s. 4   long statement 2
1 2 3 4 5 6   1 2 3 4 5 6

s. s. 5   etc.
1 2 3 4 5 6   1 2 3 4 5 6

Q1   If the melody of short statements 1 and 2 generally moves from higher to lower pitches, what is the direction of long statement 1?
a. It also descends.
b. It generally rises.
c. It stays on the same general level.
d. It rises and descends.

Q2   Which sentence best describes short statements 1 and 2 and short statements 3 and 4?
a. 3 and 4 are exactly like 1 and 2.
b. 3 and 4 are totally different from 1 and 2.

    c. 1 and 3 are exactly alike but 3 and 4 are different.

    d. 3 and 4 are very similar to 1 and 2, but there is a change in instruments.

Example 1.2   *Kusi Huaynas* (excerpt)
Traditional Bolivian music

This piece is played at carnivals and outdoor festivals (the title means *Merry Youngsters*). Several tarkas are heard playing in parallel motion throughout, accompanied by several drums (membranophones) and vocal encouragements. The song is in three sections; each section is repeated. A linking clause acts as a suffix to each musical statement. The suffix is represented by X. The song is presented twice.

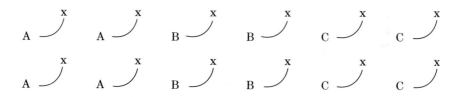

Q3   Which statement (A, B, or C) is the shortest?
    a. A
    b. B
    c. C
    d. A and C

Q4   When do the drums enter?
    a. The drums enter right away.
    b. The drums come in and out.
    c. The drums play at the very end.
    d. The drums enter soon after the song begins.

Whereas in the previous two examples the performer blows air through a chamber to reach a fixed edge, in the next two examples the performer's bottom lip is placed against the instrument (like a bottle) and a stream of air is blown directly against the opposite edge of a blowhole.

    The flute you will hear in Example 1.3 is held horizontally. The performer changes the pitches by covering the holes (in this case seven) with the fingertips. Because there are no mechanical keys on this instrument, the performer can glide from one pitch to the next by gradually sliding the finger off a covered hole.

Example 1.3   *Rag Jog* (excerpt)
             Classical North Indian music

This is an improvised solo (within the confines of a strong tradition). Notice how the flute (bansuri) frequently returns to one of the pitches heard in the background drone (sustained accompaniment).

A flute similar to the bansuri in that it is made from bamboo, is the pan flute (see Chapter 4). Named after Pan, the Greek god of shepherds, the pan flute is a series of tubes bound together to create a complete instrument. Pan flutes, in various physical configurations, are found throughout the world including China, South America, Europe, and the South Pacific Islands. Example 1.4 features yet another type of flute—the silver flute.

Example 1.4   Johann Joachim Quantz
             Concerto for Flute and Orchestra, third movement (excerpt)
             18th-century German composer

The flute is accompanied by a typical early eighteenth century orchestra consisting of violins, violas, cellos, basses, and a keyboard instrument (in this case a harpsichord). The piece is performed on a silver flute.

Q5   After the flute enters, what is the nature of the
     accompaniment?
     a. The lowest string instrument and the harpsichord are heard
        most prominently.
     b. The entire orchestra plays all the time.
     c. The harpsichord is heard alone.
     d. The strings play without the harpsichord.

As you read above, all edge instruments have one overriding similarity: the airstream is the primary vibrator. The material and the method of performance are of secondary importance. No single instrument makes this point more clearly than the pipe organ.

In comparison to the other aerophones discussed, the pipe organ is massive. Although size is not the major factor in determining its physical configuration, the organ is much too large and complex for the performer to be able to supply the air for each pipe directly. The air supply for an organ is generated by a pump and stored (constantly replenished) in a chest. As the performer depresses keys or foot pedals, the air is released to specific pipes. Like the pan flute, each pipe produces a single pitch. The pipe operates exactly like the recorder and tarka flutes—the air leaves the chest and travels through a passage to the edge of the pipe. (The organ also has pipes that have vibrating reeds.) Many other factors control the sound of the organ, which may include thousands of pipes or be relatively small.

Example 1.5   György Ligeti
                Volumina (excerpt)
                20th-century Hungarian composer

Composers are still exploring the possibilities of the organ, one of the oldest instruments in the Western world. In this work Ligeti exploits the enormous complex of sounds possible from a large pipe organ. There is no tune in the traditional sense. What we hear can

This pipe organ is massive in comparison to other acrophones.

best be described as large sound masses, which are combined like large patches of colors on a canvas.

Q6   What happens to the mass of sound?
   a. It remains constant throughout.
   b. It decreases throughout.
   c. It increases throughout.
   d. It changes throughout with both increases and decreases.
Q7   How *might* these masses of sound be performed?
   a. The masses cannot be played by the fingers and feet alone.
   b. The masses can easily be played by the fingers.

Reed Instruments

Flutes direct a column of air against a fixed edge. Reed instruments direct air against at least one *flexible* plate. The operative word is "flexible." Most reed instruments use one or two pieces of bamboo reed as the source of vibration. Most of us have placed a blade of grass between our thumbs to create our own aerophone. The grass serves as the reed, which the moving air from our lips causes to vibrate. Note that you do not have to place your lips directly on the grass (reed). That is also true of certain reed instruments, while others require the performer to place a part of the reed against the lips. Both types of reed instruments will be demonstrated in this chapter.

Reed instruments can be divided into two major groups: the double reeds (instruments that use two reeds) and the single reeds.

A double reed is created from two identical pieces of cane (bamboo or bamboo substitute), which are bound together. The reed is thin enough to be flexible and thick enough to withstand moisture and pressure. Notice that the end of the reed is not closed. This is important. After the reed is attached to the instrument the player puts about one half inch of the tip of the reed into the mouth. The reed is supported by the lips with uniform pressure to keep it from touching the teeth, slightly closing the reed.

As the player blows through the reed, it moves toward a closed position. This sends a pressure "puff" through the instrument. As the reed interacts with the air column a pressure wave travels down and back through the instrument, alternately forcing the reed toward a closed position and then to a widened position beyond the normal, rest position.

The photograph on page 22 shows four double-reed instruments used in Euro-American orchestras. They have many common charac-

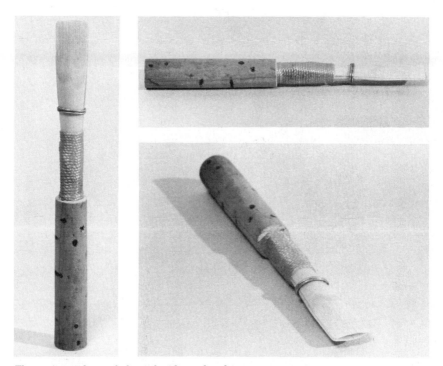

Three views of a reed: frontal, side, and end.

teristics even though they look outwardly different. They can be referred to as the oboe family.

The family of instruments related to the oboe is very large. The Western oboe, in fact, is a rather late arrival in the music world. Instruments in this extended family date back to ancient times. The aulos was a double-reed instrument used in ancient Greece. The shawn and crumhorn were used in Europe during the fifteenth and sixteenth centuries. The sona (China) and the shahnii (India) are very old members of the family that continue to be heard in the music of those two great cultures.

The bassoon and European oboe will be demonstrated later. Example 1.6 demonstrates the shahnii, an ancient non-Western oboe.

Example 1.6   *Dhun* (excerpt)
          Traditional Indian music

This Dhun, a folk piece, is performed on the shahnii, an Indian oboe of ancient and modern times. It probably originated in the

Four college students play instruments that belong to the oboe family: the oboe, the English horn, the bassoon, and the contrabassoon.

Middle East and spread to Africa, China and parts of Europe. It has six or seven fingerholes and a thumb hole. The reed is placed between both lips.

Prior to the entrance of the drum, several instruments accompany the shahnii. Listen to the example and answer the question that follows:

Q8   How many pitches are the accompanying instruments playing?
  a. Only one.
  b. Only two.

Single-reed instruments generate pressure waves in a manner very similar to that of double reeds. The vibrating agent is one flexible reed, which is bound to a rigid mouthpiece as shown in the photograph on page 24.

Members of the New York Renaissance Band with some of their instruments. Standing, left to right: sackbut, shawm, tabor. Seated: cornetto, bass gamba.

As before the player inserts the mouthpiece approximately one half inch into the mouth. The upper teeth rest on the top of the mouthpiece and the lower lip (supported by the teeth) exerts a slight pressure on the reed. The lips create a gasket around the mouthpiece so all of the air is directed into the instrument. The initial surge of air forces the reed toward the rigid mouthpiece. From this point on the

A shahnii player from India.

The parts of a clarinet mouthpiece.

A clarinet mouthpiece assembled.

reed interacts with the pressure wave that travels to and fro through the instrument, as it does in double-reed instruments.

There are two prominent families of single-reed instruments: clarinets and saxophones. The photograph below shows some standard members of the clarinet family: the soprano, bass, and contrabass clarinets.

Saxophones are shown on page 26. They will be demonstrated in a number of later examples.

Example 1.7 Darius Milhaud
Sonata for Flute, Oboe, Clarinet, and Piano
"Tranquille" (excerpt)
20th-century French composer

Each of the major families of aerophones studied in this chapter is represented in this example (flute, single reed, and double reed). A piano is also heard throughout. The instruments enter in the

These instruments illustrate various clarinets (from left to right): the contrabass, the bass, and the soprano.

Four saxophones and a clarinet (foreground).

following sequence: oboe, clarinet, oboe, flute (supported by clarinet and oboe). There is then a very brief piano solo.

Q9   Which statement best describes the sequence of entrances following the piano solo?
a. The clarinet enters, followed by the oboe.
b. The clarinet enters, followed by the flute.
c. The flute enters, followed by the oboe.
d. The oboe enters, followed by the clarinet.

Trumpet-Type Instruments

This classification includes a wide variety of instruments from many parts of the world. Only one is actually called a trumpet; the other instruments have distinctive names. They are grouped together because they have the same acoustical properties and the same technique for creating a sound. Here are but a few of the instruments that belong to this group: trumpet, bugle, conch shell, shofar, trombone, tube, euphonium, French horn, alphorn, sackbut, and cornet.

In all trumpet-type instruments the airstream is placed into vibration by the player's lips. As players "buzz" their lips the column

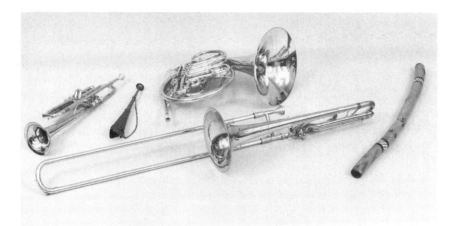

Various trumpet-type instruments from Europe, Tibet, and Australia.

of air in the instrument is pulsed by each puff of air created by the buzz. The principle is the same as described with double-reed instruments; the only difference is that the player's lips replace the vibrating reeds. While some trumpet-type instruments use fingerholes to change the length of the vibrating air column, most trumpet types utilize one of two other methods to obtain different pitches. The first method is called overblowing, as demonstrated in Example 1.8. The performer is producing every pitch with the same length of tubing, therefore the same length of airstream. The higher pitches are created when the performer tightens the facial muscles that control the lips. Tighter muscles and an increase in air pressure create higher pitches.

Example 1.8   French horn playing high pitches by overblowing

The other method of expanding the number of pitches available to the trumpet-type instrument is to change the length of the airstream. The modern brass instruments—trumpet, French horn, trombone, and tuba, the most highly developed trumpet types—change the tube length by actually adding tubing. The trombone uses a long U-shaped tube; the three other instruments use a series of valves to extend the basic length of the instrument. Each valve adds a fixed length of additional tubing. In combination the valves provide seven usable configurations of additional tubing and, as with the trombone, each new length brings another group of available pitches.

The next two examples sample trumpet types from two continents.

Example 1.9   *Twin Conch Shell Solo* (excerpt)
              Traditional Indian music

One musician is playing the two conch shells simultaneously. He holds the shells to his lips, buzzes his lips to vibrate the air within, and changes pitches by blowing harder, tightening his lips, or using his fingers to cover the shell openings.

Q10   How is the musical interest sustained throughout this example?
       a. The melody changes frequently.
       b. New rhythm patterns develop throughout.
       c. There are frequent changes in loudness.
       d. The listener's attention shifts from one conch shell to the other.

The second example of trumpet-type instruments includes representatives from the Euro-American symphony orchestral family. Each of the

This conch shell player makes music using an instrument supplied by nature. (Photograph by N. A. Jairazbhoy.)

instruments you will hear is constructed from metal (including brass) and is part of what is referred to as the "brass family."

Example 1.10   Alvin Etler
            Sonic Sequence for Brass Quintet (excerpt)
            20th-century American composer

The example opens with a French horn and is soon joined by muted trumpets, and by muted trombones playing glissandos (slides moving gradually back and forth to produce an unbroken sweep of sound).

IDIOPHONES

Tap a water glass, shake your cereal box, run your finger over the teeth of a comb, or rub your fingers on a window until it squeaks—you are creating idiophones. In each case it is the body of the "instrument" that you have caused to vibrate. Sometimes the vibration cycle is very short but as long as the vibration is strong enough to disturb the air around it and thereby set up pressure waves, you have a sound for use in a musical composition. The four "instruments" you created belong to three groups of idiophones:

1. Instruments that are struck or shaken, including bells, gongs, cymbals, and maracas
2. Instruments that are plucked, including the music box, mbira, and bowed cymbal
3. Instruments whose sound is produced by friction, including the glass harmonica

Needless to say, the world is full of potential idiophones, and they have been developed and used on every continent. The list is never-ending because new idiophones are invented every day. Steel drums, for example, were developed in the Caribbean from old metal storage barrels. They can play a full range of pitches once the tops have been stretched with a hammer or chisel.

The next two examples offer a small sampling of idiophones. Other idiophones can be heard in examples throughout the book.

Example 1.11   Robert Chappell
            Metal Anklung Solo
            20th-century American composer

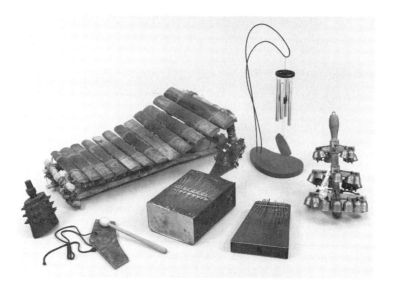

Idiophones from around the world. (Above and below.)

The anklung is a set of tuned rattles, each of which plays a single pitch. This instrument is well known in Southeast Asia where it is made of bamboo. The present example uses a rare metal form of the instrument. All of the rattles are suspended from a common rack. In Southeast Asia they are held in the hands of the performer.

Experiment with objects not normally considered musical instruments and try to create interesting sounds. Create short sound pieces using natural objects such as stones or sticks, and small machines such as a hair drier or egg beater.

Discuss the sources of music. What stimulates the act of composing?

Example 1.12   *Quiet and Beauty*
Traditional African music (excerpt)

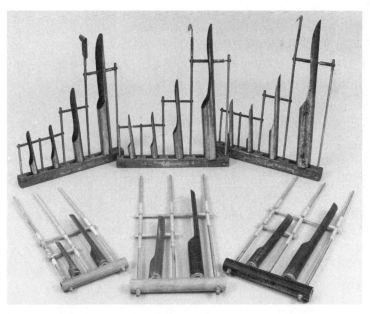

The anklung is an idiophone found in Southeast Asia. The foreground set is made from bamboo. Those in the rear are metal.

The mbira, also called the thumb piano or kalimba, is constructed from flattened nails or heavy metal wire. The metal tines are attached to a resonant box made of metal or wood and are plucked with the thumb. The pitch of each tine is determined primarily by its length. (How does length correspond to pitch?) The mbira plays a gentle, recurring melody that becomes more complicated as the example continues. The mbira is joined by a rattle and other instruments including a flute and bass. Eventually the instruments are joined by a singer.

MEMBRANOPHONES

All membranophones include a tightly stretched membrane that vibrates to create pressure waves. The membranes are usually treated animal hides or a synthetic substitute. The countless membrane drums of the world represent the largest group of instruments in this classification.

Membranophones, as the name suggests, are characterized by the membrane that is stretched over the body of the instrument.

Most drums are struck with a stick, the hand, or a mallet. Some, however, are placed into vibration by friction. Unlike the friction idiophones, it is the membrane that is caused to vibrate, not the body of the instrument. There is even a drum that is plucked. In both cases (plucked or friction) a cord or stick is attached to the membrane. The cord or stick is then rubbed and the vibrations are transmitted to the drumhead.

Other membranophones include the kazoo and the comb-and-tissue paper.

Example 1.13   Edgard Varèse
Ionisation (excerpt)
20th-century French composer

Ionisation was one of the first works written in the Euro-American concert tradition for an ensemble made up primarily of membranophones and idiophones. The composition calls for thirteen players and over forty different percussion instruments. Despite the fact that it was composed sixty years ago, it remains a very contemporary-sounding work.

Q11   Two aerophones are also heard in this example. What are they?
a. a flute and an oboe
b. a trumpet and a trombone
c. two conch shells
d. two sirens

CHORDOPHONES

Experts identify nine different categories of chordophones with ten different methods of setting the vibrating source into action. The list includes an extremely wide variety of instruments, some familiar and some not so familiar. What do chordophones have in common?

Zither, musical bow, busoi, hade, sarod, hammer dulcimer, piano, pagolo, vina, sitar, banjo, gonra, viol, guitar, lute, zheng, harpsichord, qin, psaltery, lyra, cithara, clavichord, yang qin, rebab, mandolin, balalaika, violin, harp, kasso, viola, bajo sexto . . . While it is all but certain that you cannot identify all these instruments, by examining the ones you are familiar with you will be able to deduce one common characteristic: they are all constructed by stretching one or more strings between fixed points. The strings or cords can be made from a

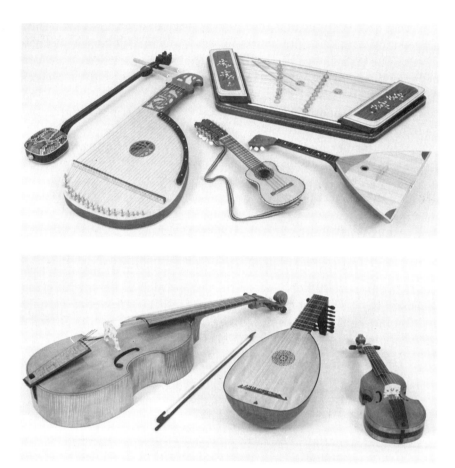

Chordophones may vary greatly in appearance, yet they share a common characteristic: one or more strings stretched between fixed points.

wide variety of materials including nylon, animal gut, metal, rubber, or other material that can be stretched and set into vibration. The simplest chordophone, then, consists of two elements: a method for holding the string firmly and a string.

You can construct a simple chordophone with a rigid board, two nails, and a piece of fishing line. If the string tension is great enough you will be able to hear a distinct pitch.

You can create a chordophone with even fewer resources. All you need is a rubber band. Find a light rubber band that when broken has a length of approximately 6 inches. Firmly grasp the ends of the rubber band with the thumb and index finger of each hand. Stretch the rubber band to a length of 12 inches and strum the band with one of your free fingers. What happens? Can you see the band vibrate? With the proper amount of tension you should be able to see several different cycles of vibration.

Very few chordophones are as simple as our "rubberbandaphone." Frequently the string is attached to a vessel, sound box, or other sound-enhancing object. Ironically, in some cases the string is probably the least important element in determining the quality of the sound produced. Vibrating strings need help to enhance projected sound. Many chordophones, such as the violin, mechanically transmit the energy of a vibrating string through a bridge into the actual body of the instrument. The bridge passes the energy of the vibrating string into the flexible body of the violin. The body, in turn, vibrates the surrounding air and enhances, or resonates, the sound. Without the carefully crafted violin body, the string would create a pale sound.

For convenience, since the variety of chordophones is so great, the following discussion divides these instruments into two large families: instruments with changeable string length and instruments with fixed string length. (Other systems of classification are possible and equally valid.)

Family One: Changeable String Length

Anyone familiar with the violin or guitar will recognize this family of instrument. With each, the performer changes the length of the string by depressing the string against a fingerboard or fret, respectively. The contact with the board or fret stops the string from vibrating on the portion behind the hand. The shorter the string the higher the pitch.

During the next example a violin is joined by a guitar. The guitar is picked or strummed by the fingers or a plectrum. The violin can be bowed by a ribbon of horsehair or plucked.

Example 1.14   John McLaughlin   *electronic*
                Dream (excerpt)
                20th-century American composer

The violin and guitar are heavily modified by electronic processors in this example. Are you able to identify any of the other instruments used?

Q12   How are the violin strings set into vibration?
    a. only by plucking
    b. mostly by plucking but also bowed briefly
    c. only by bowing
    d. mostly by bowing but also plucked briefly

Example 1.15 demonstrates a different approach to changing string length. The zheng heard in the example is a zither from China. The koto from Japan is also a zither. The string length of these two zithers can be changed in two ways. In the first method, the bridge that supports the strings is moved. The performer plucks and strums the zheng with the right hand. Therefore the length of the sounding string extends from the right edge of the instrument to the bridge. The farther the bridge is placed from the right edge the longer the string is and the lower its pitch.

In the second way, the player depresses the portion of the string to the left of the bridge with the left hand. When the string is depressed the tension of the string increases. What will happen to the pitch?

The zheng, a Chinese instrument, is a zither and, of course, a chordophone.

The koto is a zither from Japan.

pentatonic

Example 1.15   *Wild Geese Alighting on the Sandy Shore* (excerpt)
Traditional Chinese music

The zheng is joined by the hsiao, a vertical flute made from bamboo.

Family Two: Fixed String Length

This family of instruments includes the piano, harpsichord, and harp. If you have ever looked inside a piano you will have noticed that metal strings are stretched and supported by a heavy metal frame. The weight of the frame is determined by the amount of stress created by the stretched strings. Other chordophones require less string mass and tension and are therefore less massive. A harp, for example, uses a wooden frame. The piano's strings are struck by padded hammers controlled from an elaborate mechanical keyboard. The vibrating strings pass their energy into a soundboard, which in turn sets the air

The interior of a piano prepared by John Cage. Here he has used spoons, nuts and bolts, screws, and other small objects.

in and around the piano into motion. Without the soundboard and large surrounding case for resonance, the piano would have a pale sound.

Example 1.16   Henry Cowell   *keyboard*
Banshee (excerpt)
20th-century American composer

Instead of using the keyboard, the performer leans into the piano case, scraping and striking the strings. The sound is intended to represent a banshee, a spirit in Irish folklore whose wailing foretells a death. Does the fact that the keyboard is bypassed in favor of direct contact with the strings remove this instrument from the chordophone family?

Explore the recordings in your library. Seek out sounds you have never heard and make their acquaintance.

Experiment to see what sounds a piano can produce without the use of the keyboard.

Visit a rehearsal of one of the performing groups at your school. Listen to the characteristic sounds produced on instruments used. Take note of what seem to you special effects or unusual sound combinations.

The harpsichord, heard in Examples 1.1 and 1.4, is related to several other chordophones. The performer uses a keyboard with its various mechanical connections, like the piano, but the similarity stops there. The strings of the harpsichord are plucked by quills or leather plectra. The sound is very different from that of the piano.

Example 1.17   Johann Sebastian Bach
Goldberg Variations, "Aria" (excerpt)
18th-century German composer

Explore other chordophones in the library record collection. You will find an exploration of harps and the hammer dulcimer very rewarding since these two instruments are found in numerous cultures throughout the world.

ELECTROPHONES

An electrophone produces sound through a loudspeaker by means of a vibrating cone, like a membranophone. The speaker vibrates in a pattern that simulates or is analogous to the actual pattern of the original sound. To make a simple comparison: A flute creates a pressure wave, a microphone "hears" the wave and converts it to an electronic entity. An amplifier directs this electronic information to a speaker which in turn moves air. Electronic instruments skip step one. Complex circuits create electronic patterns that are passed directly through the speaker. The electronic patterns are electronic

Although this electronic music studio reflects modern technology, many comparisons can be made to traditional instruments.

analogues of synthesized sounds. Oscillations of voltage replace oscillations of air.

In many cases we cannot see an electrophone in action in the same way that we can observe a pianist. Keyboard electrophones activate circuitry inside the instrument that operates at the molecular level.

The world of electronic music is far too vast to explore in any detail here. The advent of the digital computer has created a firestorm of instrument development. Some of the earliest electronic instruments, the ondes martenot and the theremin, were developed in the 1920s. Recording tape was not available until after World War II, and synthesizers were not used until the 1960s. Today we hear electronically generated music nearly every day. Electronic instruments are now heard in concert halls, on the recordings of concert, jazz, and popular music artists, and as movie and television background music. Radio and television commercials are dominated by electronic instruments. We are in the age of electronics, but whether we are at the beginning, middle, or end of the electronic revolution cannot be stated with certainty. It is probably safe to speculate that we are witnessing only the beginning and can look forward to an ever more rapid and refined development of electronic instruments.

Example 1.18   Mitchel Forman
             Odd Angel
             20th-century American composer

This example demonstrates the flexibility of electronic instruments. New instrumental sounds are created that share characteristics with some of the aerophones, chordophones, membranophones, and idiophones already heard in this chapter. Some electronic composers strive to imitate existing instruments, while many composers strive to create new instrumental sounds. Nearly every instrument in this example has been produced electronically.

SYNTHESIS

This final section of many of the chapters will present a complete small piece by way of summarizing the topic of each chapter. Sometimes, as here, it will not be possible to encompass every aspect of the topic. As we have seen, our sound environment is too vast for any single piece to represent more than a small sample.

Example 1.19   Harry Partch
             *Barstow—8 Hitchhiker Inscriptions from a Highway Railing
             at Barstow, California,* "Number 1"
             20th-century American composer

Few compositions could serve as well as *Barstow* to represent our multifaceted sound environment, for it combines the fruits of a noted composer, an honored craftsman, and a modern acoustical experimenter—all in the person of Harry Partch. Drawing on cultures past and present for his models and materials, Partch built all his own instruments so that he could get the kinds of sound he wanted. You will hear four of these instruments in this work. The two idiophones, the diamond marimba and the boo (a bamboo marimba—listen for its low snapping sounds), are both African in origin; the chromelodeon, an aerophone, is an adaptation of the European reed organ, with Partch's own special tuning; and the surrogate kithara, a chordophone, is based on a strummed and plucked string instrument of ancient Greece. To this eclectic combination Partch has added a text for speaker and singer taken directly from the graffiti of American hobos.

Harry Partch playing the boo.

"Number 1" is divided into two parts. Part 1 begins with an instrumental introduction, followed by six lines of spoken text that are occasionally enhanced by a sung background. Part 2 is the sung portion. Here are the words of each part:

PART 1

"Number One."

1. "It's January twenty-six."
2. "I'm freezing."
3. "Ed Fitzgerald, age nineteen, five feet ten inches, black hair, brown eyes."
4. "Going home to Boston, Massachusetts."
5. "It's four p.m. and I'm hungry and broke. I wish I was dead."
6. "But today I am a man."

PART 2

1. "Going home to Boston—uh huh—Massachusetts."
2. "It's four p.m. and I'm hungry and broke. I wish I was dead."
3. "But today I am a man."
4. "Oh—I'm going home to Boston—uh huh—Massachusetts."

The instrumental introduction is played by the diamond marimba and the chromelodeon. The diamond marimba continues as the primary accompanying instrument throughout the spoken section.

Q13   During which line in Part 1 does the chromelodeon return?
    a. line 1
    b. line 4
    c. line 5
    d. line 6

During Part 1 the singer joins the speaker and sings "Going home . . ." several times. Each time he sings this phrase he is accompanied by the kithara and the boo. Listen to these instruments again.

Q14   How many times is the phrase "Going home . . ." interjected in Part 1?
    a. five times
    b. eight times
    c. four times
    d. three times

Q15   Which two instruments are played most often during Part 2?
    a. diamond marimba and chromelodeon
    b. boo and diamond marimba
    c. chromelodeon and kithara
    d. kithara and boo

Q16   Which instrument is used only as a form of punctuation or emphasis in Part 2?
a. chromelodeon
b. kithara
c. boo
d. diamond marimba

Q17   How many instruments are used in Part 2?
a. one
b. two
c. three
d. four

OUR SOUND ENVIRONMENT

The Human Voice

In one sense, the classification of the human voice is much simpler than that of other musical instruments. Traditionally, the voice is most frequently classified by its relative highness or lowness of pitch (register). The most frequently used terms for register are listed below, from highest to lowest:

Female:	soprano	high register
	mezzo-soprano	middle register
	alto (or contralto)	low register
Male:	tenor *Pavarotti*	high register
	baritone	middle register
	bass	low register

Coloratura
– ultra high
higher than
soprano

Castrati – high young male voice

Know

The classification of a voice, however, is more complicated than merely assigning a register. Each voice within a single register group shares other characteristics—the most important of which is resonance, or richness of sound.

Example 2.1 demonstrates the four principal registers: soprano, alto, tenor, and bass.

Example 2.1   George Frideric Handel
               Messiah, "And with His stripes we are healed"
               18th-century German composer

The title of this chorus, "And with His stripes we are healed," includes all the words sung. Each time, the main entrances of this sentence consist of the following pattern of short and long durations:

short short short long
and   with his   stripes

And each time, a different voice type presents the words. Practice saying this short—short—short—long pattern several times, and then follow the main entrances of the voices, the sequence of which appears below. Listen to the example until you can detect each entrance.

soprano	tenor	bass
alto	bass	soprano
tenor	alto	bass
bass	soprano	
soprano	alto	

Each member of this choir has a unique sound but tries to blend with other voices.

THE VOCAL MECHANISM

From the purely physical standpoint, the method of sound production appears to be a simple phenomenon. Air stored in the lungs is caused to flow through the vocal cords, two parallel and flexible folds of muscle located in the larynx. As the cords vibrate they create a series of air pulses, a process that is analogous to a trumpet player's buzzing lips. As a matter of fact, the sound produced by the vocal cords has a buzzing quality. It is what happens to the sound as it travels toward the mouth that makes discussion about the human voice so complicated. The fact is that while the sound of every voice is initiated in an identical fashion, scientific measurements have confirmed that no two voices are totally alike. So the classification of the human voice is not such a simple matter: there are as many different vocal instruments in the world as there are people.

While singing and speech have a number of important differences, it is their similarities that can help us understand how the voice works. The specific sound of an individual's voice—its timbre or tone color—is a combination of two interactive forces: genetics and conditioning. Genetics controls the physical aspects of the voice. The size and shape of a singer's mouth, teeth, throat, tongue, lips, nasal cavity, sinuses, and bone density, which are all-important in the shaping of his or her individual vocal timbre, are determined by genetics. The way the singer uses these physical aspects is a learned or conditioned behavior. Both the young child and the opera singer learn by copying a desired model. With the child the learning is almost unconscious, but the opera singer requires talent, the proper physical attributes, and a concentrated period of focused training. The difference is one of degree, however, since the tasks are similar.

Back to genetics. Have you ever called a friend on the telephone and carried on a conversation before you discovered you were talking to his brother or father (assuming your friend is a postpubescent male)? Of course most families have a similar way of pronouncing words, and a common vocabulary and speed of speech, but the similarity runs deeper. As we have seen, all parts of the vocal mechanism are genetically shaped. The more similarly shaped the voice mechanism, the more similar the voice. The singer can control only certain parts of the vocal mechanism. The controllable elements include the proportion of air flow through the mouth and nasal cavity through manipulation of the soft palate and the tilt of the larynx. The singer can also alter the shape and placement of the tongue in relation to the teeth and palate and the shape of the lips (from tightly pursed to widely spread). The genetically inalterable elements are the hard tissues, such as the hard palate, the nose, and the sinuses. These give the voice its family signature.

The voice finds its expression in a wide variety of contexts and settings. It may be very soft, as soft or softer than speech, as in a mother's lullaby; it may be very loud, loud enough to be heard above an instrumental ensemble of more than ninety instruments. The softness of a mother's lullaby or the loudness of the singer competing with instruments is appropriate to their musical context and setting. There are many beautiful voices in the world. In part their beauty is measured in relation to how appropriate they are to the task at hand. The following discussion about vocal power, then, is not intended to suggest that more is better. More is simply different from less, and beautiful voices can be found at all points along the continuum.

VOCAL POWER

Singing loudly is very hard work. A great amount of air must pass through the vocal mechanism, supported by a complex set of muscles and bones, to create a loud sound. The entire torso must be highly energized. Singers who earn their living singing loudly, such as opera singers, must be in top physical condition to expend the amount of energy required to sing a demanding opera role. Rarely do opera singers perform two nights in a row. They simply cannot sustain the physical effort.

With the popularity of amplified concerts and recording, the relative power of an individual voice is somewhat obscured. All recorded music operates within a narrow range of loudness, a range dictated by the equipment and materials used to record and play back the music. Live, amplified concerts are also misleading. Your favorite singer may only whisper into a microphone but the loudness, due to a powerful amplification system, may match that of a newly airborne 747. The only real way to measure the power of a voice is by hearing it without amplification. (But be aware that standing too close to a very loud singer can actually hurt your ears.)

Interesting things happen when singers increase their loudness. Examples 2.2 and 2.3 demonstrate two distinctly different approaches to vocal power by two singers, both models in their respective fields.

The amount of physical energy used to project their voices is very different. The singer in Example 2.2 has a voice suitable for folk or pop music. He sings with a very relaxed approach. He uses a microphone and sings at a level that is not much louder than a lecturer's voice. The singer in Example 2.3 specializes in opera and sings *very very* loudly. The process of recording and playback makes the two selections sound as though they are of equal loudness but that is an illusion. Listen to the two examples several times and answer the question below.

 Example 2.2   Michael Kamen and Marty Fulterman
              Beside You (excerpt), 1970
              20th-century American composer/performer

The singer in Example 2.2 sings very close to the microphone. One barely perceives the energy being expended to produce the tone. The two high points of the song are on the words *"beside you"* and *"sunrise."* The increase of energy needed to sing the highest pitches is hardly noticeable.

Placido Domingo and John Denver are examples of opera and folk singers.

Example 2.3   Gustav Mahler   *Domingo*
The Song of the Earth, "Drinking Song of Earth's Sorrow"
(excerpt), 1908

This example opens with an orchestral introduction. The singer sings three times during the example. Each time he sings he is accompanied by a rather full orchestral accompaniment. The singer sings three distinct melodies. Notice the strength of the voice. Try to duplicate the physical sensation that one would have in singing both examples.

Listen to both examples again.

Q1   Which singer is singing with the most physical exertion?
a. the opera singer in Example 2.3
b. the folksinger in Example 2.2

Q2   Which singer is closest to the microphone?
a. the opera singer
b. the folksinger

Listen to the amount of energy the opera singer uses in the three successive passages. Compare the three passages.

Q3   Which passage requires the greatest amount of energy?
a. the first
b. the second
c. the third
d. They are the same.

EXPRESSIVE DEVICES

Singers use a variety of techniques to enhance the expressive context of their voices. Three common (but not universal) techniques are 1) glissando (often called portamento), in which the singer slides up or down to a pitch; 2) ornamentation, in which the singer superimposes a brief melodic flourish on a pitch, such as ⎯⋀⋁⋀⎯ ; and 3) vibrato, in which the singer periodically fluctuates the pitch. We will not explore the first two devices. You should attend to those techniques on your own. As you learn to identify them, keep in mind that you are merely identifying what is present.

Vibrato

Vibrato is a periodic fluctuation of pitch. If we represent pitch by a straight line: _____, vibrato would look something like these variations:

A.

B.

C.

Two major factors are in play: 1) the speed of the fluctuation, which can actually be measured in terms of oscillations per second, and 2) the range of frequency change from the highest to lowest pitch. The three representations of vibrato above all have the same rate of speed, but (A) reflects the greatest range deviation. A further variable is the consistency or constancy of the vibrato:

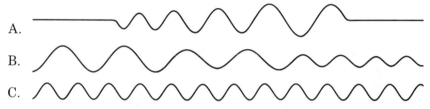

A.

B.

C.

(A) represents a straight pitch to which is applied vibrato that increases in range and slows in rate. Finally the pitch straightens out again.

(B) demonstrates a fairly slow vibrato that first gets slower and narrower in range and then increases in speed but decreases in range.

(C) represents a vibrato that is regular in rate throughout its duration. It is not as wide in range as (A) and not as narrow as the end of (B).

Since standards of vibrato and its use vary greatly, all we can usefully do is describe a vibrato in such relative terms as slow-moderate-fast; very narrow-moderate-wide; or fixed-variable.

Let's go back to Examples 2.2 and 2.3. You can hear the vibrato used in Example 2.2 primarily at the ends of each line. Actually, there is only a faint suggestion of vibrato used. Most of the time the singer sings without a noticeable vibrato. When the vibrato is noticeable it is slow and shallow. The vibrato seems suitable to the simple message of the song and serves merely to "warm" the voice on certain words. It is certainly not an important factor in this piece.

The vibrato used in Example 2.3 is very noticeable. The singer uses vibrato throughout the example. It is traditional for opera singers to use vibrato all of the time. The vibrato seems to intensify during the most dramatic moments of the example. We can use these two examples as a basis of comparison with the other vocal examples in this book.

Q4   What is its relative speed?
    a. slow to moderate
    b. moderate to fast
    c. fast to very fast

Q5   What is its relative range?
    a. very narrow
    b. moderate to wide
    c. very wide

Example 2.4   John Dowland
Come Again (verses 1 and 2)
16th/17th-century English composer

We hear a mezzo-soprano (a middle-range female voice) accompanied by a lute (a chordophone with a fretted fingerboard). Compare this approach to vibrato with earlier examples.

Q6   How does the speed of vibrato compare with the singer in Example 2.3?
    a. The vibrato is slower.
    b. The vibrato is somewhat faster.
    c. The vibrato is much faster.

Q7   Is vibrato used throughout the example or only at times?
    a. It is used sparingly.
    b. It is used only on important words.
    c. It is used throughout.

Example 2.5   Woody Guthrie
John Henry (excerpt)
20th-century American composer/performer

In this ballad the performer is most interested in having the listener hear every word. Little effort is made to enhance the melody. A second voice provides harmonic support.

Woody Guthrie

Q8 How is vibrato used?
   a. Very little vibrato is used.
   b. A great deal of vibrato is used.
   c. Certain words have a very distinctive vibrato.

THE WORD

Speech

Remember that the sound of a natural voice is greatly influenced by genetics. On the other hand, our speech patterns are greatly influenced by our environments. We learn to speak by imitating those around us, as our regional American accents clearly indicate. The Southern drawl, for example, elongates vowels and suppresses final consonants. Other regional accents shift the stress syllable in a word. For example, some Americans pronounce the word *Detroit* with an accent on the first syllable: DEEtroit. You will have no trouble thinking of many other examples.

The differences that mark a singing voice are most noticeable in the vowels (*a, e, i, o, u*) and diphthongs (complex sounds of more than one vowel sound gliding into another, as in the word *boy*). The vowels hold the key to understanding the singing voice. We sing on vowels. Vowels are the source of resonance (richness of tone) and the key to understanding vocal timbre.

Diction

We learn our speech patterns naturally, but singers have a cultivated or studied approach to words. Vocal diction is very different from speech. A person raised in Texas can, through the study of vocal diction, sing convincingly in many languages. Every musical style (pop, classical, country western, blues, jazz, etc.) has its own rules of diction.

We have all been delighted by the ability of actors and impersonators to mimic the speech patterns of another person. Actors usually adopt an accent that indicates a national origin or social status. For example, fans of the gifted American actress Meryl Streep have heard her give convincing performances portraying such diverse characters as an Australian, a Pole, a poor Southern laborer, and an upper-class Britisher. Rich Little, the famous impersonator, is a master of imitation. He, unlike Streep, imitates specific individuals. How do they achieve these marvelous deceptions?

One very important component in imitating or cultivating a chosen vocal quality is the placement of the sound. We all have a great deal of control over the location of our vocal sound within the vocal mechanism. Sing the vowel sound in the word *eat*, but keep your lips together; now try to move your voice to various parts of the vocal mechanism. Try these different manipulations, still singing *ee* with your lips together:

1. Open your jaw as far as you can and relax your tongue.
2. Push your tongue against the roof of your mouth.

The difference should be dramatic. During the first sound, the tone resonates through the entire throat and the oral and nasal cavities. During the second sound, by constricting the space, you made the tone resonate primarily in the front of the mouth and the nasal cavity. Singers can control this placement by, among other techniques, adjusting the openness of their jaw. Some singing styles require a barely opened mouth, while other styles require a maximum opening of the jaw.

It's fun to listen to different voices and try to replicate the techniques the singers are using to produce the sound. Try this with the next four or five singers you hear. Where are they placing the sound?

Once artists like Streep and Little capture the right placement or tone quality for a particular voice they want to imitate, they have to master the diction patterns of the imitated voice. Diction for the singer involves enunciation, pronunciation, and articulation (the way sounds are connected). The field of diction is much too complicated to describe here, but there are a number of simple diction elements we can examine that will help you have a more involved listening experience:

1. Are the initial consonants (those at the beginning of words) and the closing consonants emphasized or suppressed?
2. Is the sound of the vowel modified or intact?
3. What is the timing of the diphthongs? That is, is the first or the second sound sustained? (Diphthongs, remember, are a combination of two or more vowel sounds, as in *boil* or *sour*.

Consonants: Say the word *help* five times, each time pronouncing the *H* less and less:
HELP   ⊦ELP   ⊦ELP   I ELP   ELP
The continuum is from emphasis to suppression.

Now pronounce the word *car* as printed here:
CA   CAr   CAR   CARR
The size and number of R's indicate the range from suppression to emphasis. Singers make this kind of choice all the time.

Vowels: The classic case is the word *tomato,* which can be pronounced TO-MAY-TO, TO-MAH-TO, or even TO-MAY-TA.

Diphthongs: Here again the question is one of emphasis, which is extremely important in singing. Whether a singer emphasizes the first or the second sound in a diphthong is very much a matter of who the singer is and the context or vocal style in which he or she is singing.

Examples 2.6 and 2.7 illustrate a number of these differences in the approach to vocal diction. These two songs, "Just You Wait" and "The Rain in Spain," are from Lerner and Loewe's *My Fair Lady,* a musical adaptation of Bernard Shaw's *Pygmalion.* There are two main characters: Eliza Doolittle, a young woman from lower-class London, and Henry Higgins, a professor of phonetics (diction), who feels he can transform Eliza into a lady by teaching her to speak (and in this case sing) with proper diction. Example 2.6 is the *before;* Example 2.7 is the *after.*

 Example 2.6   Alan Lerner and Frederick Loewe
My Fair Lady, "Just You Wait" (excerpt)
20th-century American composers

Two verses of the song are included on the recording. Listen to the first verse several times:

Line 1:   "Just you wait, Henry Higgins, just you wait!
Line 2:   You'll be sorry but your tears will be too late.
Line 3:   You'll be broke and I'll have money.
           Will I help you? Don't be funny!
Line 4:   Just you wait, Henry Higgins, just you wait!"

Line 1 has several changes in the diction that are calculated to imitate a cockney accent. The diphthong in the word *wait* is modified to sound more like *white.* Notice also that the H in *Henry* and *Higgins* is gone: a case of consonant suppression.

The three types of modification described above (of consonants, vowels, and diphthongs) are present in line 2. The word *sorry* has an unusual emphasis on the final *ee, will* has the *w* suppressed, and *late* (like *wait*) changes the sound of the diphthong so the word is similar to *light.*

In line 3 the H in *have* and *help* is gone. The word *don't* sounds more like *doun't.*

If you say the following sentence as written you will be on your way to a cockney accent:

Just you white, 'enry 'iggins, just you white.

A scene from the musical, *My Fair Lady*

Now listen to the first and second verses together. Here is verse 2:

Line 1: "Just you wait, Henry Higgins, till you're sick,
Line 2: And you screams to fetch a doctor double quick!
Line 3: I'll be off a second later and go straight to the theater.
Line 4: Ha ha, Henry Higgins, just you wait!"

How many more diction changes can you find in this verse?

Example 2.7   Lerner and Loewe
               My Fair Lady, "The Rain in Spain" (excerpt)

This is the song of triumph when Eliza Doolittle proves that she can now pronounce the English language like a "lady." Blatant chauvinism aside, it is a delightful idea. The words are simple enough:

"The rain in Spain stays mainly in the plain."

How would Eliza have sung this line before her diction "makeover"?

Example 2.8   James Taylor
             Never Die Young (excerpt)
             20th-century American composer/performer

Luckily Henry Higgins never met James Taylor or many of the other thousands of vocal individualists. It's productive to think of all the different voices of the world as being unique threads in the fabric of music. Both voices of Eliza Doolittle were charming. One does not negate the other.
The words to *Never Die Young* follow:

Line 1:   We were ring-around-the rosy children
Line 2:   They were circles around the sun
Line 3:   Never give up, never slow down
Line 4:   Never grow old, never die young
Line 5:   Synchronized with the rising moon
Line 6:   Even with the evening star
Line 7:   They were true love written in stone
Line 8:   They were never alone, they were never that far apart
Line 9:   And we who couldn't bear to believe they might make it
Line 10:   We had to close our eyes
Line 11:   Cut up our losses into doable doses
Line 12:   Ration our tears and sighs

Listen to this example until you can sing along with it. Then turn your attention to the following questions, which are designed to heighten your musical perception as it relates to a singer's diction and style.

Q9   What word in Line 1 features an elongated or stretched vowel sound?
      a. we
      b. ring
      c. children

Q10   The word *never* is heard four times in Lines 3 and 4. How many clearly pronounced final **r** sounds do you hear?
      a. one
      b. two
      c. three

X **Q11** During Line 7 one word is altered dramatical̲ from normal speech rhythm. What is the word?

    a. were

  X b. written

    c. stone

Q12 There is a somewhat long pause between two words in Line 8. The pause is between which of the following pairs of words?

  a. they/were

  X b. were/true

    c. never/alone

Q13 The word *never* is heard twice during Line 8. Is the final **r** more audible on the first or the second *never*?

  X a. the first

    b. the second

Q14 James Taylor is joined by other voices during two of the final four lines. Which two feature more than one voice?

    a. lines 9 and 10

    b. lines 9 and 11

    c. lines 10 and 11

  d. lines 10 and 12

SOUND AND WORDS: SOLO OR ENSEMBLE

Throughout most of the chapter we have separated the sound of the voice from the words in order to understand each component more clearly. The last three examples will bring the two parts together as we briefly study the differences between solo and ensemble vocal music.

The opening example in this chapter features a large vocal ensemble: a choir of male and female voices. As you will remember, the text for this piece was "And with His stripes we are healed," and you heard thirteen separate entrances of it. The text refers to the Christian belief that Christ suffered and died so humanity's sins could be forgiven. Listen to Example 2.1 again. Do you hear individual voices? You don't, because in choral music the desired effect is to make each individual voice blend with all the others. That loss of individuality has its compensations, however. Singing as a unit, the choir gains power in the sense that it represents everyone. The sound and the words are a unified whole to which the individual is subordinate.

A vocal solo, on the other hand, allows for a great deal of word and sound variety. Because it is easier to understand the words of a single singer, the solo voice can sing more complex vocal lines and communicate a more elaborate text than a choir.

Example 2.9   Durval Ferreira/Pedro Camargo/Ray Gilbert
                 The Day It Rained (excerpt)
                 20th-century South American and North American
                 composers

Besides being a master of the use of vibrato, Sarah Vaughan, the American jazz singer heard here, also uses a wide variety of other vocal techniques to enhance the expressive qualities of this composition. Among other techniques, she uses glissando (the sliding from one pitch to the other) and modification of consonant and vowel sounds as a form of creative alteration that heightens the musical interest. This exercise will require great concentration.

Listen to *The Day It Rained* very carefully as you follow the words. Answer the questions that follow the lines of the lyrics:

Line 1: "Rain, you gentle rain, now that you're on my window pane."

Q15   During line 1, Vaughan uses vibrato on the word *rain* in two
       different ways. How do they differ?
       a. The first *rain* has vibrato throughout; the second *rain* has no
          vibrato.
       b. The first has no vibrato; the second does.
       c. The first has a steady vibrato; the second begins with no
          vibrato but adds it later.
       d. The first begins with no vibrato and adds it; the second has
          continuous vibrato.

Line 2: "Before you go, will you explain something for me?"

Q16   During line 2, what word is begun without vibrato but gradually
       adds it?
       a. before
       b. go
       c. something
       d. me

Line 3: "Rain, I wonder why today there's such a different sky."

Sarah Vaughan

Line 4: "It isn't raining rain, it's teardrops that I see."

Q17   During line 4, there is a glissando (slide) between two words.
What are the words?

    a. it—isn't
    b. raining—rain
    c. it's—teardrops

Line 5: "Are you sad because you know my heart no longer sings?"

Q18   What words in line 5 conclude with a short descending glissando?

    a. You/know
    b. sad/because
    c. heart/sings
    d. sad/heart   better of a · b are

Line 6: "It's like a bird trying to fly with broken wings."

Q19   What word in line 6 receives a significant amount of
       ornamentation?
       a. bird
       b. fly
       c. broken
       d. wings

Line 7: "Rain, my love is gone, but the memories remain."
Line 8: "So maybe that's why the sky is so gray."

Q20   What word features a vowel exaggeration in line 8?
       a. why
       b. sky
       c. so
       d. gray

Line 9: "You heard his goodbye when he walked away."
Line 10: "Now both of us cry recalling the day it rained."

Q21   What word features a descending glissando in line 10?
       a. us
       b. cry
       c. it
       d. rained

The final two examples of this chapter are for large groups of
singers. They are very different than the solo you just heard, a solo full
of individualism—a celebration of the solo voice.

Example 2.10   Johann Sebastian Bach
                Mass in B Minor, No. 3: "Kyrie" (excerpt)
                18th-century German composer

The entire text is "Kyrie Eleison" ("Lord, have mercy"). The first
four entrances are in this sequence: bass, tenor, alto, soprano. Even
though all the voices are singing the same words they never
(during this excerpt) sing them together. The words, for one brief
moment in the piece, are printed below to show the four different
simultaneous treatments of the text (a dash indicates that the
previous syllable continues):

Soprano	i	—	son	e	le	—	i	—
Alto	son	—	ky	—	—	—	ri	—
Tenor	son	—	e	—	le	—	—	—
Bass	i	—	son	e	le	—	i	—

How does the text retain its intelligibility? Because there are only two words the meaning is made clear before the second voice enters. The voices are free to weave an intricate, interlocking pattern without losing the meaning of the words.

There are several ways of experiencing such a piece. Try the following:

1. Listen to the excerpt four times. Each time follow one voice part throughout. (It won't be easy.)
2. Listen again and try to hear all the parts at the same time, but focus on the moments when *Ky* and *son* are sung.

The first way will help you develop your ability to focus on one element in a complex context: an important skill. The other will help you recognize beginnings and endings of musical ideas: also an important skill. No single method is superior as long as you maintain your focused concentration throughout.

Chapters 1 and 2 have described our sound environment, the colors used to create musical compositions. In the remaining chapters we will learn how composers and performers create their compositions and how we can learn to become involved listeners.

OUR
TIME
FRAME

Like all the elements of music, time is more easily experienced than discussed. Every composition is a unique realization of time—not the time of the clock, in which five minutes is always 300 seconds, but the kind of psychological-experiential time in which five minutes can seem to flash by in no time or can seem to last for an eon. All music exists within this experiential time frame, but particular compositions move within it in two distinctly different ways: some music moves with an even pulse that marks off regular segments of time, while other music moves freely, with no discernible sense of pulse at all. Example 3.1 illustrates the first of these ways; Example 3.2 illustrates the second. Both of these examples were heard in Chapter 1.

Kaou X   **Example 3.1**   Johann Sebastian Bach
                      Brandenburg Concerto No. 4, first movement (excerpt)
                      18th-century German composer

Q1   What instrument(s) create(s) a steady pulse?
X a. harpsichord
  b. recorders
  c. violins
  d. harpsichord and bass

Know   **Example 3.2**   György Ligeti
                      Volumina (excerpt)
                      20th-century Hungarian composer

Both these types of movement in musical time have something to
do with time in nature and in everyday life. The second type has
some parallel in those uneven happenings—an unexpected visitor,
a sudden shower, for example—that cut across the steadier
rhythms of nature and life's daily routines. The first type seems

Paintings exist in space just as music exists in time. Which is the "real" space here—the
40″ × 30″ of the frame or the endlessly rolling vista within it? (*Stone City, Iowa,* 1892, by
Grant Wood)

directly related to our ordinary activities, which we measure with agreed-upon units of time, such as seconds, minutes, days, and weeks. Though based in nature, these man-made units reflect our apparent need to regulate and keep track of where we have been and where we are going. Comparable units in all musics of the world appear to mirror the same need, suggesting some tie to our primordial roots—or even, beyond them, a link between musical time and cosmic rhythms. Whatever the case, mystical or mundane, we do respond to time in music in very active and direct ways. Whether consciously or unconsciously, we sense how time—along with other musical elements—creates the effects of tension and repose that are central to our response to music. *Tension* and *repose* are terms we will be using from now on, and you will understand more and more about their nature as we proceed.

PACE

Pace can be defined as the rate of activity for any musical element, perceived in relation to some norm. Once a general level of activity has been established, any increase or decrease in the *rate* at which sounds change is a change of pace. In general, increasing the pace of any element tends to increase the level of tension—speeding up the pulse, making sounds louder or softer than an established level, changing the quality of sound, and so on. By the same token, decreases in the rate of any of these activities tend to lower the level of tension toward more repose. In the following examples various kinds of change of pace are present.

Example 3.3   Franz Schubert
Piano Quintet ("Trout"), first movement (excerpt)
19th-century Viennese composer

There are three distinct sections in this excerpt. The pace increases progressively from section to section, from the slow motion of the opening to the more rapid pace during the violin solo and the still faster pace during the piano solo. The solos themselves can be perceived as the norm, against which the increases in pace are supplied by the accompaniment.

Example 3.4   John Coltrane
A Love Supreme (excerpt), 1964
20th-century American composer/performer

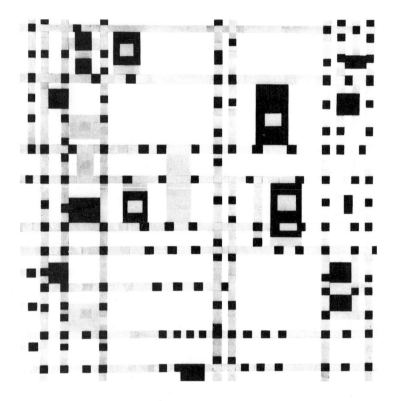

Does one of these paintings seem to you to have a greater sense of pulse than the other? And can you see a change of pace in either of them? (Above: *Broadway Boogie Woogie,* 1942–43, by Piet Mondrian, below: *One (Number 31, 1950),* 1950, by Jackson Pollock. Sydney and Harriet Janis Collection Fund (by exchange). Collection, The Museum of Modern Art, New York.)

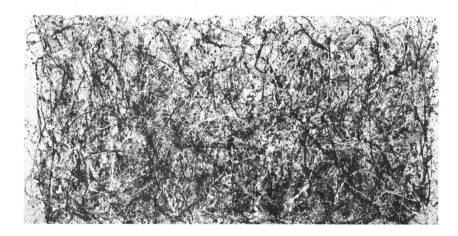

Changes in pace here coincide with the points of greatest tension. As the solo develops, Coltrane slowly adds more and more activity to the constant background of drums, bass, and piano, achieving the greatest tension by playing higher pitches at a faster pace. The greatest levels of repose are created by slowing the pace and playing relatively lower pitches.

Example 3.5   Alvin Etler
               Sonic Sequence for Brass Quintet (excerpt)
               20th-century American composer

This example (which you heard in Chapter 1) incorporates two alternating levels of pace. One is significantly faster than the other.

Q2   How does the pace in the last section relate to the pace in the previous section?
      a. It is the same pace.
      b. It is a slower pace.
      c. It is a significantly faster pace.

TEMPO

Steady Tempo

In the Ligeti excerpt (Example 3.2), musical events unfold in a kind of free flow, without recurring regularity. In the Coltrane (Example 3.4), we hear familiar instruments and gestures of the jazz tradition, yet the strong steady sense of pulse we expect is obscured. And because our expectations are denied, the tension level is raised. This often happens in our musical experience and in our daily experience as well. You will certainly be inclined to make a more foot-tapping response to Example 3.6 than to either the Ligeti or the Coltrane. With expectation more nearly fulfilled, the general level of tension will likely be lower.

Example 3.6   Sonny Rollins
               I Got It Thad (excerpt)
               20th-century American composer/performer

In this piece, as in a great many others, you can find at least two pulse rates with which to tap along: one moderately slow, and one twice as slow as that. You will probably decide that the moderately slow rate asserts itself as the basic pulse.

The basic pulse rate defines the *tempo* of a piece. Thus, the more basic pulses there are within a given time span, the faster the tempo, and vice versa. There are no absolutes in describing tempo as fast or slow. As a rule of thumb, tempos close to a normal heart rate (72 to 76 pulses per minute) can be considered moderate; tempos on either side are relatively slower or faster. (It is possible, of course, for a composer to indicate a tempo precisely by giving performers the specific instruction of a metronome marking: a certain note value at a certain rate per minute.)

Example 3.7   Akira Miyoshi
Concerto for Orchestra, first movement (excerpt)
20th-century Japanese composer

As in the Sonny Rollins piece, you can find two pulse rates here—one very fast and one half that fast. Because nearly all parts move insistently at the very fast pulse rate, it tends to dominate and become the basic pulse, creating a very fast tempo.

Changes in Tempo

In both the preceding examples the tempo, once underway, proceeded steadily. Almost unconsciously we tend to expect this steady state as a norm in a piece of music, and thus changes in tempo intrude strongly on our awareness and tend to produce repose or tension. There are four common kinds of tempo change:

1. an abrupt shift in basic pulse rate
2. a gradual increase in basic pulse rate *(accelerando)*
3. a gradual decrease in basic pulse rate *(ritardando)*
4. a constant give-and-take in basic pulse rate *(rubato)*

We can show them graphically, like this:

basic pulse	□ □ □ □ □ □ □ □ □ □ □ □
abrupt shift	□ □ □ □ □ □ □ □
accelerando	□ □ □ □ □ □□□□□□□□□
ritardando	□ □ □ □ □ □ □ □ □
rubato	□ □□□□ □ □ □ □□□□ □ □ □ □

Since any change in a basic pulse rate is so easily perceived, composers and performers use tempo changes for a variety of important effects, such as signaling a new mood or the beginning or end of a musical idea. For these effects, accelerando and ritardando can help provide a smooth transition, while an abrupt tempo change tends to have a dramatic effect, heightening tension or lowering it suddenly. Speeding up or slowing down, particularly in the give-and-take of rubato, can be used to intensify the impact of a musical idea. Examples 3.8–3.12 illustrate different kinds of tempo change, sometimes more than one in a single example.

Example 3.8 Ludwig van Beethoven
Symphony No. 1, first movement (opening)
18th/19th-century Viennese composer

This excerpt has two distinct sections. This first opens with a series of sustained sounds in which it is almost impossible to sense a pulse, though the tempo is steady and the pace slow. Soon, however, the violins begin a melody with a definite pulse that confirms the slow tempo. The second section changes to a faster tempo, and the rate of activity—the pace—likewise increases.

Q3 Which of the four kinds of tempo change is used?
    a. an abrupt shift
    b. a gradual increase in basic pulse rate (accelerando)
    c. a gradual decrease in basic pulse rate (ritardando)
    d. a constant give-and-take in basic pulse rate (rubato)

Example 3.9 Dmitri Shostakovich
Symphony No. 5, fourth movement (opening)
20th-century Russian composer

Like Example 3.8, this excerpt has two sections. The beginning is a bold statement by brass and timpani, later punctuated by woodwinds and string. The second section is primarily for strings. Listen to the tempo change that begins the moment the timpani drop out.

Q4 Which of the four kinds of tempo change is used?
    a. an abrupt shift
    b. a gradual increase in basic pulse rate (accelerando)
    c. a gradual decrease in basic pulse rate (ritardando)
    d. a constant give-and-take in basic pulse rate (rubato)

Clap of tempo (handwritten)

Example 3.10   Hector Berlioz
Symphonie Fantastique, first movement (excerpt)
19th-century French composer

There are two basic tempos, one for each of the two main sections.

Q5   What is the relationship between the two tempos of this example?
    a. One is pulsed and the other is not.
    b. The first is faster.
    c. The first is slower.

Q6   How does Berlioz change tempo from the first to the second
    section?
    a. with rubato
    b. with a ritardando
    c. with an accelerando

Example 3.11   Frédéric Chopin
Nocturne, Op. 55, No. 1 (excerpt)
19th-century Polish composer

The tempo can be determined by following the lowest pitches in the
left-hand part.

Q7   Which of the four kinds of tempo change is used here?
    a. abrupt
    b. accelerando
    c. ritardando
    d. rubato throughout

A Javanese gamelan at Northern Illinois University. Note the number and variety of
gongs and xylophones.

Example 3.12 *Sekar Vled*
Balinese music

This music is played by a Balinese gamelan, an orchestra consisting of bronze gongs of various sizes and metal, wood, and bamboo xylophones. After the first few sounds a steady tempo is set. There are two tempo changes near the end of the example.

Q8 How would you describe the two tempo changes?
   a. an abrupt shift followed by a rubato section
   b. an accelerando followed by a ritardando.
   c. a ritardando followed by an abrupt return to the original tempo
   d. a ritardando followed by a rubato section

Try to find two or more performances of the Chopin nocturne in Example 3.11 and compare the interpretations. Do they all change tempo in the same place? in the same way?

See if you can find different performances of the introduction to the first movement of Beethoven's *Symphony No. 1* (Example 3.8). Compare the tempos, with the help of a metronome if possible. Which interpretation strikes you as the most effective?

Pace and tempo are two of the ways in which musical events are organized within the broad framework of time in music. Together with meter (Chapter 4) and the manipulations of meter to form patterns in time (Chapter 5), they make up *rhythm* in its broadest sense. All aspects of rhythm play a fundamental part in generating effects of tension and repose. Some of these effects have already been mentioned, and they will receive more and more attention in chapters to come.

SYNTHESIS

Example 3.13 will help you discover how changes in tempo and pace can interact in a complete piece. We will concentrate on these three things:

   1. changes in tempo

2. changes in pace
3. differences in pace between the two voices

Example 3.13   Giuseppe Verdi
Rigoletto, "Love Is the Flame" *(È il sol dell' anima)*
19th-century Italian composer

The first part of the piece is for solo tenor voice. Here is the Italian text, with the lines numbered for easy reference:*

1. È il sol dell' anima, la vita è amore;
2. sua voce è il palpite del nostro core,
3. e fama e gloria, potenza e trono,
4. umane, fragil qui cose sono;
5. una pur avvene, sola, divina,
6. è amer che agl' angeli più ne avvincina!
7. Ah! Adunque amiamoci, donna celeste,
8. d'invidia agli uomin sarò per te,
9. d'invidia agli uomin sarò per te.

During the second part the tenor is joined by a soprano. Since the texts of the two are mixed and often repeat in fragments, the duet section will be represented graphically. Each horizontal line stands for an entrance; the line-numbering scheme is continued.

10. Soprano begins   _____ ____
    Tenor joins later   _____
11. Soprano continues   _____
    Tenor joins for conclusion   _____
12. Tenor begins   _____ _____
    Soprano joins   ____   ____ ____
13. Soprano begins   _____   _____
    Tenor joins   _____   _____
14. Together   _____
15. Vocal cadenza (passage of
    vocal display) together   _____

The basic tempo of the piece is established by the orchestra at the beginning. The pace is set by the rate of change in the text. At the start, there are either one or two syllables on each pulse. The

*Translation: "Love is the flame which fires our souls. Its voice is the beating of our hearts. Fame and glory, power and throne are but human frailties. Such joy not even angels can emulate. Ah! Love me, then, and I shall be the most envied of men."

following questions will help you discover changes of tempo and pace throughout the composition.

Q9   Most of the lines in the first part of this example demonstrate at least one type of tempo change. What line of the tenor solo (lines 1–9) has no tempo change?
a. 1
b. 3
c. 5

Q10   Which word in line 7 is subjected to the greatest change in tempo?
a. Adunque
b. Ah!
c. donna

Q11   In lines 2 and 4 a single word (different in each line) is treated elaborately through ornamentation (the pace increases). What are the two words?
a. del, qui
b. sua, umane
c. core, sono

Q12   Which of the lines during the tenor solo has the greatest change of pace, that is, the largest number of syllables per pulse?
a. line 8
b. line 7
c. line 6

Q13   Does the pace of the orchestral accompaniment increase or decrease from line 9 to line 10 (at the beginning of the soprano passage)?
a. It increases.
b. It decreases.

Q14   Which line during the duet (lines 10–15) has the least ritardando?
a. line 12
b. line 13
c. line 14

Q15   Is the pace at the beginning of line 12 faster or slower than in line 11?
a. faster
b. slower

Q16   In lines 10–15, during which line does the soprano move at a faster pace then the tenor?
a. line 13
b. line 14

RHYTHM: METER

BUILDING BLOCKS
Meters in Twos or Threes

Like the human pulse, musical pulse is a series of undifferentiated impulses all of equal length and emphasis. But in music that has pulse (as we have seen, not all music does), we usually perceive the pulses in groups of two or three. Our sense of these groupings results from a stress or accent—real or imagined—at the start of the first pulse of each group. *Meter* is the marking of musical time by these two-pulse or three-pulse units. Thus, if you clap to the rate of your heartbeat with equal emphasis on every clap, you are simply clapping pulses, but if you clap *strong*-weak or *strong*-weak-weak you are creating two-pulse or three-pulse meters. These small units can operate separately or they can become building blocks of other, larger metrical groupings.

Examples 4.1 and 4.2 illustrate three-pulse meters; Example 4.3 and 4.4 illustrate two-pulse meters. In each example, the tempo is determined by the basic pulse rate.

Example 4.1   Giuseppe Tartini
Symphony in A Major third movement (excerpt).
Early 18th-century Italian composer

The tempo of the basic three-pulse group is quite fast, with the beginning of each *strong*-weak-weak group emphasized by low sounds in bass:

*Diagrams like this one are a handy way to illustrate meter groups, and they will be used regularly from now on. Each square represents a single pulse; pulse groups are shown by the vertical lines; and the accented pulse is shown by the symbol >. In multiline diagrams, the line showing the *basic pulse* is preceded by the abbreviation BP.

Example 4.2   Johann Sebastian Bach
Mass in B Minor, "Et incarnatus est" (excerpt)
18th-century German composer

After a brief introduction, five different entrances from each section of the choir clearly outline the three-pulse meter. The sequence of entrances is: alto, soprano, high soprano, tenor, and bass. Each separate entrance begins on the strong pulse of the metric group. The tempo is very slow.

Example 4.3   Franz Joseph Haydn
Symphony No. 94, second movement (excerpt)
18th-century Viennese composer

As in Example 4.1, the bass instruments emphasize the metric organization of this example. In most metric groupings, the second pulse is silent or unaccented. Listen for the *strong*-weak grouping of the two-pulse meter.

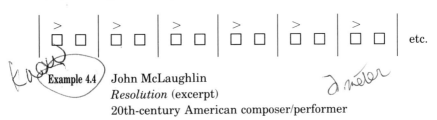

Example 4.4   John McLaughlin
Resolution (excerpt)
20th-century American composer/performer

The tempo of the basic two-pulse group is moderate. It is partly defined by the snare drum which puts a strong accent on the second pulse of each group; this is a simple form of *syncopation*—the unexpected absence or displacement of the normal first-pulse accent that defines the basic meter group. This kind of metrical conflict is one of the most common tension-raising devices in music, and we will pay more attention to it later in this chapter. In the following diagram the upper line shows the *strong*-weak two-pulse group with the accent that defines it; the lower line shows the conflicting snare drum accent.

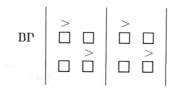

Although the meter of a piece is often described only in terms of the basic pulse group, there are almost always pulse groups at more than one level, sometimes at several levels simultaneously. In listening to Example 4.1, for instance, you may have noticed a good deal of activity in the violins at a pulse rate twice as fast as that of each basic pulse. Put another way, this faster level of meter results from dividing each basic pulse into two parts. The basic level and its subdivision can be diagrammed like this:

In *Resolution* (Example 4.4), pulse groups can be heard at four levels, as in this diagram:

As you can see from the diagram, the pulse rate in *Resolution* doubles at each of the faster levels. At the slower level we can sense a grouping of each pair of basic pulses into a longer time unit consisting of a single pulse.

Now listen to Examples 4.5–4.7. Find and tap out all the meter levels in each, deciding first which pulse is the basic one, and then answer the question for each example.

Example 4.5   Roger McGuinn and Gram Parsons   *3 meter*
Drug Store Truck Drivin' Man (excerpt),
20th-century American composers

Know own clap

Q1   At the basic level, are the pulses grouped by twos or threes?
a. twos
b. threes

Example 4.6   Wolfgang Amadeus Mozart   *2 meter*
Horn Concerto No. 4,
third movement (excerpt)
18th-century Viennese composer

Know own clap

Q2   At any level faster than the basic one are the pulses grouped by twos or threes?
a. twos
b. threes

The Doge's Palace, Venice. Can you see how its pattern of arches strikingly resembles some of the diagrams in this chapter?

our—class

Know

Example 4.7   Scott Joplin
          Maple Leaf Rag (excerpt)   *two meters*
          20th-century American composer/performer

Q3   Is there more than one pulse level heard in this example?
       a. no
       b. yes

In many pieces the composer emphasizes stability by keeping the pulse groups at each level consistent throughout an entire piece, or within a major section of a large work. In other pieces, changing the pulse groups from twos to threes or vice versa results in a heightening of rhythmic interest, an increase or decrease in tension, or—as in Example 4.8—a special emphasis on certain words of the text.

Example 4.8   Claudio Monteverdi
          L'Orfeo, Act 1
          "Leave the Mountains, Leave the Fountains"
          16th/17th-century Italian composer

The first section, in a moderate tempo, has groups of twos at all levels, thus:

The second section shifts to a basic pulse group of threes at a faster tempo, emphasizing a reference to dancing in the text. The third section (instruments only) carries on the tempo and basic meter of the second. In both these sections you can hear a second metric level that joins two of the basic three-pulse groups into longer two-pulse groups:

An interesting shift in metrical grouping occurs at the end of the instrumental line (heard twice). Two threes are regrouped into three twos:

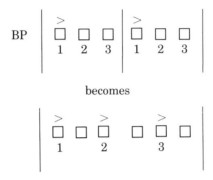

becomes

This effect, called *hemiola,* can be found frequently in music as far apart in time and style as a medieval religious song and the tune "America" from *West Side Story.*

Meters in Twos *and* Threes

Except for the hemiola effect just described all the examples so far have had a basic pulse group of two *or* three consistently maintained, marking off equal time spans. In many pieces unequal time spans are created by mixing twos and threes, a procedure that tends to raise the level of tension for two reasons: (1) our musical conditioning leads us to expect that time will be marked off equally, and any expectation denied is a source of tension, and (2) such mixtures are harder to keep track of than consistent repetition of a single basic pulse group.

Example 4.9 provides a classic example of a 3 + 2 metric grouping. During the eighth metric group (of 3 + 2) you will hear the pipes enter on the two-pulse portion of the group.

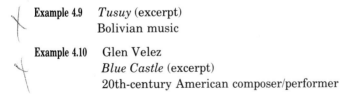

Example 4.9   *Tusuy* (excerpt)
              Bolivian music

Example 4.10   Glen Velez
               Blue Castle (excerpt)
               20th-century American composer/performer

The meter in this selection has seven beats arranged 2+2+3. The seven beats move at a moderate rate. You will hear approximately seventeen sets of seven beat measures. By the way, it would be equally correct to hear fourteen beats if you count at the faster strokes of the drum.

The example opens with a hand drum and is followed by a shaker, an additional drum and finally the solo instrument, a piano. The piano is accompanied by several sustaining wind or wind simulated instruments, but these instruments do not contribute to the metrical feel of the composition. A diagram of the entrances is shown below. Follow each measure. You will have to listen to the excerpt several times before you'll be able to follow the meter. Listen for the shaker entrance after the first fourteen beats. The shaker plays the seven beat pattern throughout the excerpt. Once the piano enters you will recognize a consistent pattern that is marked by greater activity during beats four, five, and six.

Measure One: Hand drum
Measure Two: Hand drum continues
Measure Three: Shaker enters (seven clear beats)
Measure Four: Second drum enters
Measures Five and Six: Single line piano melody
Measures Six and Seven: Piano with added single pitch accompaniment
Measures Eight and Nine: Piano melody with added part
Measures Ten and Eleven: Piano with sustained background
Measure Twelve: Piano alone
Measure Thirteen: Piano with harmonic and other sustaining instruments
Measure Fourteen to end: Piano with sustained instruments

Sometimes equal and unequal time spans are woven together; small unequal spans can be repeated to produce larger spans of equal length, as in Example 4.11.

Example 4.11   Dave Brubeck
                Three to Get Ready (excerpt)
                20th-century American composer/performer

changing meter example

Following the piano introduction, which has four groups of three threes, there are two statements of the same musical material. Each statement has four clearly distinct sections; each section, in turn, has a pattern of 3 + 3 followed by 2 + 2 + 2 + 2. The first statement begins with the saxophone in threes, the second statement with the piano.

Example 4.12   Dave Brubeck
            Blue Rondo Alla Turk (excerpt)

In this piece Brubeck uses a somewhat more complex pattern
than in Example 4.11. It consists of nine pulses: 2 + 2 + 2 + 3
played three times, followed by 3 + 3 + 3. The complete pattern of thirty-six pulses is thus made up of four equal nine-pulse
groups.

Example 4.13   Don Ellis
            Turkish Bath (excerpt)
            20th-century American composer/performer

This work begins with sitar and tamboura (two Indian string
instruments), in a pulseless free flow in time. At the end of this
opening section the sitar is joined by the band in a 2 + 2 + 3
pattern. The tempo is moderate, the pulse groups are well marked,
and you should be able to clap the pattern easily.

Ravi Shankar playing the sitar.

Create metrical "sentences" of two-pulse and three-pulse "words" in different orders. Perform the sentences by tapping them out.

Select phone numbers at random and form them into metrical groups with proper accents. Divide any digit higher than 3 into pulse groups of two or three. The phone number 325–7523, for example, would divide like this:

```
3    2     5              7              5      2    3

3 + 2 + (3 + 2) + (2 + 3 + 2) + (2 + 3) + 2 + 3
         or            or           or
       (2 + 3)     (2 + 2 + 3)     (3 + 2)
                      or
                  (3 + 2 + 2)
```

Are some phone numbers more interesting than others? Why?

If you have listened and clapped enough to follow the patterns presented so far you will enjoy trying to cope with the more complex patterns of Example 4.14.

Example 4.14   Don Ellis
New Horizons (excerpt)
20th-century American composer

After the brief beginning passage the piece falls into a fast 17-pulse pattern that becomes easier to pick up as the work progresses. The pattern is first grouped as (3 + 2) + (3 + 2) + (2 + 2) + 3, repeated four times, and then as (2 + 3) + (2 + 3) + (2 + 2) + 3, again repeated four times.

Invent short pieces for homemade percussion instruments, contrasting events flowing freely in time with events that have a regular pulse.

METRICAL CONFLICT AND AMBIGUITY

Examples 4.15–4.22 illustrate three types of metrical complication—*syncopation, superimposed subdivision,* and *suppressed* meter—that always create conflict or ambiguity, or both, and thus always increase the level of tension whenever they are used.

Syncopation

Syncopation and the tension-raising potential of its unexpectedly absent or conflicting accents was defined and illustrated earlier in this chapter (Example 4.4). Examples 4.16 and 4.17 offer further evidence of syncopation's unmistakable effect.

Example 4.15   Peter Ilich Tchaikovsky
Swan Lake, "Valse" (excerpt)
19th-century Russian composer

[handwritten annotations: "Klba cleos"; "+ triple meter good example"]

The normal accent of the fast three-pulse basic meter (heard after the introduction in the basses) is contradicted by repeated stress on the second pulse of the group (in the upper strings). The basic pulse continues simultaneously with the syncopation.

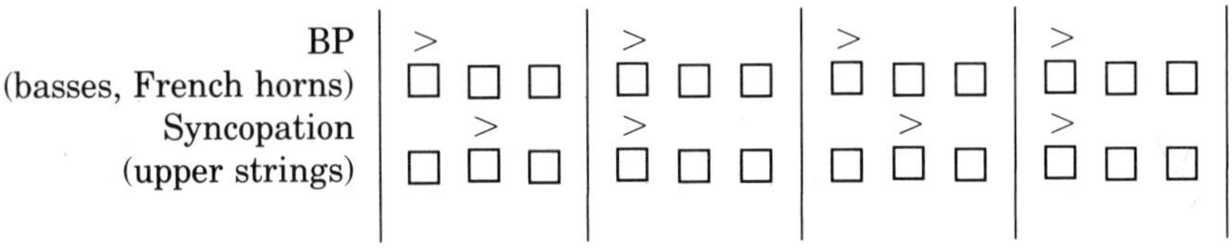

	>			>			>			>		
BP (basses, French horns)	□	□	□	□	□	□	□	□	□	□	□	□
Syncopation (upper strings)	□	> □	□	> □	□	□	□	> □	□	> □	□	□

About midway through the example a solo flute is heard above the syncopated figure in the upper strings. It plays at a faster subdivision than the basic pulse.

Q4   Is the flute part syncopated?
a. yes
b. no

Example 4.16   Traditional Bolivian music
Kusi Huaynas (excerpt)

This example of Bolivian folk music played on tarkas was heard in Chapter 1. The tarkas are played at outdoor festivals from late December to the beginning of Lent. The music is highly syncopated. If you tap your foot along with the background beat you will notice that the tarkas are almost always off of the beat

Example 4.17   Aaron Copland
             Music for the Theatre, first movement (excerpt)
             20th-century American composer

Many syncopated rhythms carefully placed together can create great excitement for the listener. At times in this example the syncopations become so complex that it is nearly impossible to distinguish the basic pulse group.

Superimposed Subdivision

Superimposing a new subdivision on a well-established meter level always creates metrical conflict—thus raising the level of tension—because it increases the number of musical events the listener must deal with simultaneously. The device is seldom used throughout a piece, since its effectiveness lies in the surprise of contrast the added subdivision provides to what has preceded it. Listen for this contrast in Example 4.18–4.20.

Steel band music is noted for its metrical intimacy and sophistication. Shown here, steel drum player, Bobbie Kingsley, performs at the Annual West Indian Day festival in Brooklyn, New York.

Example 4.18   Franz Shubert
               Piano Quintet ("Trout"), first movement (excerpt)
               19th-century Viennese composer

In this example, there are at least three levels of subdivision. The violins introduce the basic pulse near the beginning. Later in the example, you may sense a shifting of the basic pulse to a faster level. Each time you listen to the example—and you should listen to it at least three times—try to feel the pulse and its various subdivisions.

Example 4.19   *Sutileza* (excerpt)
               Traditional Cuban music

This is a fascinating example of superimposed meter. The basic rumba pattern (3 + 3 + 2) is superimposed against the basic two-pulse meter. Placed against that is a syncopated figure in the claves (a high-pitched idiophone, two wooden dowels struck together).

	>		>		>		>	
BP	□	□	+□	□	□	□	+□	□
rumba pattern	> □ □ □	> □ □	> □ □	> □ □	> □ □	> □ □	□	
claves	> □ □ □	> □ □	> □ □	> □ □	> □	> □	□ □	

Over this background, the bongo-drum player plays complex patterns in strong conflict with the basic meter. The effect is so powerful that you may find it difficult to pay attention to the voices and orchestra. An additional element that raises the level of rhythmic excitement in this example is the melody (first introduced by the muted trumpet) creating a pattern of three pulses within the same time as the basic two-beat pulse group.

Example 4.20   Charles Ives
               Symphony No. 3 (excerpt)
               20th-century American composer

Charles Ives is noted for his complicated use of superimposed subdivisions. This example shows how much tension can be created in music through this technique. While the basic pulse remains constant throughout the excerpt, our attention shifts from instrument to instrument as they create conflicting metrical groupings.

Suppressed Meter

Suppression of strong metrical emphasis often leads to ambiguity and the sort of uncertainty that is always a source of musical tension. The device has long been used in Western music in styles as drastically different as a sixteenth-century Mass (Example 4.21) and a twentieth-century orchestral work (Example 4.22).

Example 4.21   Josquin des Prez
Missa Ave Maris Stella, "Christe eleison"
16th-century Flemish composer

Here any sense of regular metrical grouping is minimized by the staggered entrances of the voices and their continuous rhythmic independence. Each musical idea is marked by syncopated figures that create shifting accents at irregular intervals.

Example 4.22   Claude Debussy
The Sea (La Mer), second movement (excerpt)
19th/20th-century French composer

There are several metrical patterns in this excerpt, but none emerges as the dominant one, largely because there is little contrast of loudness and softness and, therefore, little or no accentuation of metrical groups. Debussy may have deliberately kept the meter flexible to capture the fluid rhythms of the sea.

SYNTHESIS

Sometimes a piece will include passages built on a single pulse group—twos or threes—as well as passages that combine twos and threes either successively or in superimposition. Example 4.23 illustrates this kind of metrical complexity.

Example 4.23   John McLaughlin
Open Country Joy
20th-century American composer/performer

There are three clearly defined sections in this piece. The third resembles the first, while the second is in strong contrast. The opening section begins with most of the rhythmic activity at two widely separated rates of speed, one quite slow (the bass), the other quite fast (other instruments).

Q5 Are the main pulse groups of the bass twos or threes?
    a. twos
    b. threes

Q6 At the fast level of activity (mostly electric piano and snare drum),
    how many pulses are there to each main bass pulse?
    a. two
    b. three
    c. unequal groups of twos and three

Soon after the beginning, a violin solo starts.

Q7 Is the rate of rhythmic activity (pace) of the solo faster, slower, or
    the same as the fast pulse rate of the beginning?
    a. slower
    b. faster
    c. same rate

Q8 Are there any sections of the solo itself that lack metrical
    definition?
    a. no
    b. yes, the high tones
    c. yes, the low tones
    d. yes, the long-held tones

The second section begins after a rather long silence.

Q9 At the outset, and several times thereafter, a new pulse rate comes
    into play. Does it quicken or slow the pace?
    a. It quickens the pace.
    b. It slows the pace.

Q10 Does the bass continue with its original slow pulse group, or shift
    to a faster, syncopated figure?
    a. It continues with the original slow pace.
    b. It shifts to a faster syncopated figure.

The third section begins right after the end of the second, with no
intervening silence.

Q11 Does the overall rate of rhythmic activity shift gradually or
    abruptly at the beginning of this section?
    a. It doesn't change.
    b. It shifts gradually.
    c. It shifts abruptly.

Q12   Is the pulse rate of the violin solo generally the same as in the
      first section, or does it mostly coincide with the faster rate of other
      instruments?
      a. It is the same.
      b. It mostly coincides with the faster rate.

Using a diagram like the ones we have employed in this chapter to
represent pulse groups and levels of meter, try to outline the
relationship between the slow bass pulse and the fast pulse of
drums and piano in the first section.

Q13   How many levels of two-pulse metric groups can you find between
      these extremes?
      a. one
      b. two
      c. three

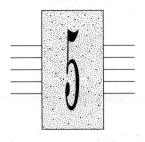

RHYTHM: PATTERNS IN TIME

Rhythm, as traditionally defined, takes in everything that has to do with the organization of musical elements in time. In this large sense rhythm is as much a part of music without pulse as it is of music with its pulses grouped into metric arrangements like those in Chapter 4. Rhythm includes pace, tempo, meter, and—beyond meter—an almost infinite number of ways in which long-short durations of sound and silence make up patterns in time. Here we will concentrate on a few simple examples of these rhythmic patterns in time, and for the purposes of this chapter, the terms *rhythm* and *rhythmic pattern* are used interchangeably.

Sometimes the rhythmic pattern and the basic pulse of a piece of music are almost identical, as in the opening phrases of "Twinkle, Twinkle Little Star":

BP

> □	□	> □	□	> □	□	> □	□
Twin-	kle	twin-	kle	lit -	tle	star.	
How	I	won-	der	what	you	are.	

Except for the word "star" in the first phrase and "are" in the second, rhythm and the basic pulse coincide.

Try tapping the basic pulse of a familiar tune with your foot and clapping the rhythm of the words. Sometimes (as in "My country, 'tis of thee," for example) the pulse and the rhythmic pattern of the words will coincide almost as closely as in "Twinkle, Twinkle." But if you tap the basic pulse of "Old Folks at Home," you will discover that there is a considerable difference between the pulse and the rhythmic pattern of the words. The foreground of the rhythm is heard and felt against the background of the metric pulse group, setting up a tension between rhythm and meter that is one of the most common sources of rhythmic interest:

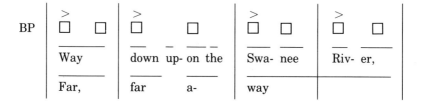

BP

> □	□	> □	□	> □	□	> □	□
Way		down	up- on the	Swa-	nee	Riv-	er,
Far,		far	a-	way			

For all but one word, the normal spoken accents of the words coincide with the metrical accent or, in the case of "-on," the strong part (beginning) of an unaccented pulse. The exception, of course, is "riv-er." Its second syllable, never accented in speech, receives a double stress: its length, and the fact that it is syncopated—it falls on an unaccented part of the pulse. In calling attention so strongly to a weak syllable, the composer disrupts our expectations and sets up the kind of tension between meter and rhythm that we noted in several examples in Chapter 4. In "Old Folks at Home" the tension is relaxed at the end of the second line by having metrical accent and normal word accent coincide on "a-*way*."

RECOGNIZING RHYTHMIC PATTERNS

Rhythmic patterns are an important factor in musical organization because they are one of the chief means of providing both tension and repose. A sense of repose generally results when some one element supplies unity by remaining unchanged while other elements are undergoing significant modification. For instance, if the pitch of a musical idea is being changed while the rhythm remains clearly identifiable, the stability of the rhythm provides a norm for the listener that holds the tension down. On the other hand, when a rhythmic pattern is subjected to considerable variation (other elements aside), the unpredictability of the variation and the larger amount of information the listener must absorb can generate a great deal of tension. Naturally, if you as the listener cannot clearly identify a rhythmic pattern, you will have no way of knowing if the pattern remains unchanged or if it is varied, and you will thus miss the effect of these changing tension levels. All the examples in this chapter are designed to develop your ability to recognize rhythmic patterns.

Unique Patterns

We will begin by concentrating on how rhythmic patterns function in brief passages, leaving until a later chapter the larger contexts in which these patterns figure prominently in providing unity and variety. In the following examples you will be asked to do two things: to match the rhythmic pattern you hear against one of the given diagrams, and to compare that pattern with the music that follows it. (Occasionally you will be asked other kinds of questions too.) Concentrate on the rhythmic pattern, not the pitches. You will find it helpful, once you have identified the correct pattern, to practice until you can tap it fluently.

> **Example 5.1**   Ludwig van Beethoven
> *Piano Concerto No. 5* ("Emperor"), first movement (excerpt)
> 18th/19th-century Viennese composer

> **Q1**   Which line in the diagram on the next page matches the full
> orchestral entrance after the brief piano introduction?
> a. line 1
> b. line 2
> c. line 3

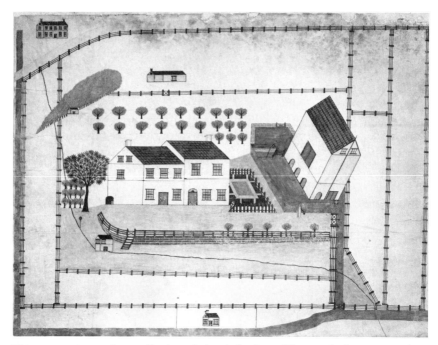

This picture is a unique collection of visual rhythms. What analogies can you draw between its rhythms and musical rhythms? (*Pennsylvania Farmstead with Many Fences.* Early 19c., anon.)

Q2 After the basic pattern is played by the full orchestra the clarinet has a solo. How does the rhythm of the clarinet part compare with the rhythm of the orchestral section?

a. It is identical.

b. It is very similar but not identical.

c. It is contrasting.

Example 5.2   *John Henry* (excerpt)
                American folk music

Q3   Which line in the following diagram matches the beginning of the
      first verse after the guitar introduction?
      a. line 1
      b. line 2
      c. line 3

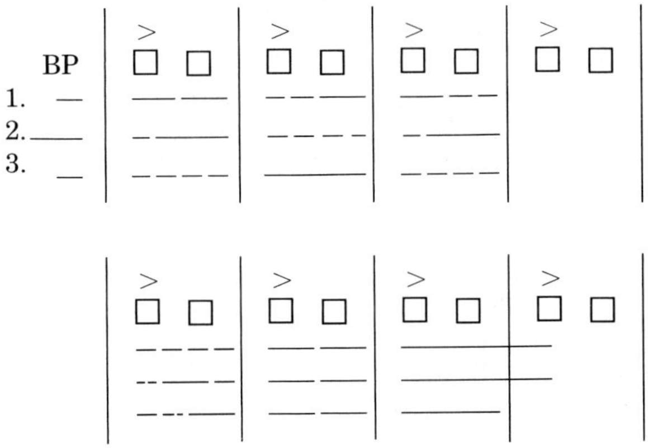

Q4   Is syncopation present in the excerpt?
      a. yes
      b. no

Q5   How does the rhythm of the second verse compare with that of the
      first?
      a. It is an identical repetition.
      b. It is a similar, but varied pattern.
      c. It is a completely contrasting rhythm.

The basic pattern of the excerpt begins with an upbeat (or *pickup*)
on the word "John," which gives a sense of falling forward to the
first accented pulse ("*Hen*-ry"). The special lift a pickup provides is
a feature of many rhythmic patterns. If you didn't notice the effect
of the pickup, you may want to listen again.

Example 5.3   Johannes Brahms
                Variations on a Theme by Haydn (excerpt)
                19th-century German composer

This example contains six musical statements in this order:

1. statement 1
2. statement 2
3. statement 1 repeated softer

4. statement 2 repeated louder
5. statement 3
6. statement 4

The following questions deal with the rhythmic pattern of the first statement, and the relationship between it and the other statements.

Q6   Which line in the following diagram matches the rhythm of the first statement?

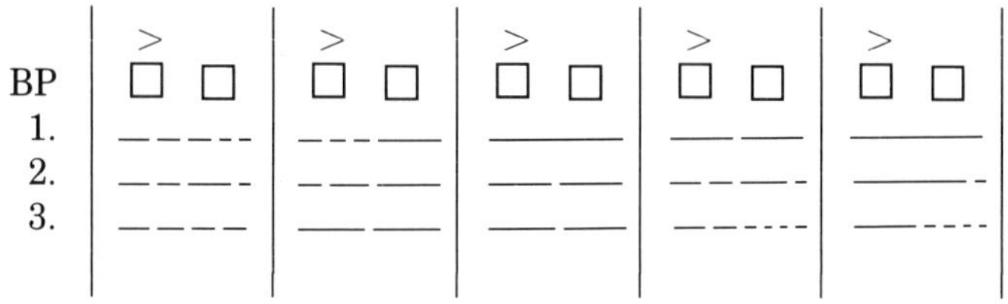

a. line 1
b. line 2
c. line 3

Q7   How does the rhythm of the second statement compare with that of the first?
a. It is rhythmically identical.
b. It is the same, but with a difference at the beginning.
c. It is the same, but with a difference at the end.
d. It is different.

Q8   How does the rhythm of the third and fourth statements compare with that of the first and second statements?
a. It is in contrast.
b. It relates to the end of the first statement.
c. It relates to the beginning of the first statement.

Example 5.4   Carole King and Gerry Goffin
              Snow Queen (excerpt)
              20th-century American composers

The vocal line begins with two short sections that are almost like a statement and response. Most of the excerpt is in this statement-response format. The tempo of the basic pulse is slow.

Q9   Which line in the following diagram matches the first statement and response in the vocal line?

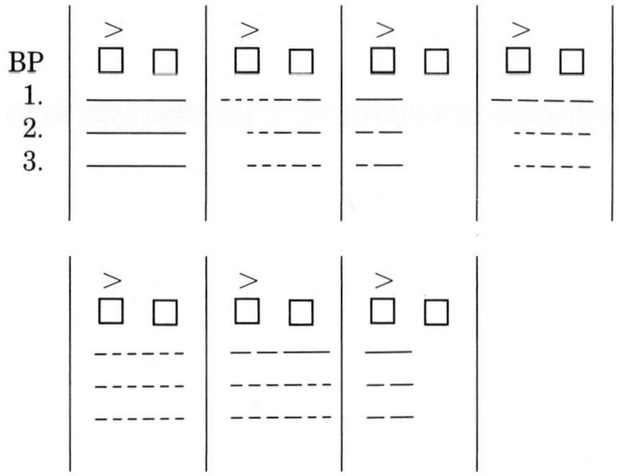

a. line 1
b. line 2
c. line 3

Q10 In the vocal line, is syncopation present in just the statement or in both statement and response?
a. in just the statement
b. in both statement and response

Q11 Is the second vocal statement and response rhythmically identical to or different from the first?
a. different from the first
b. identical to the first

Q12 In the vocal line, the pulse groups shift from twos to threes. Is the instrumental accompaniment consistently in twos or consistently in threes?
a. consistently in twos
b. consistently in threes

Example 5.5   Wolfgang Amadeus Mozart
               Piano Concerto No. 24
               first movement (opening)
               18th-century Viennese composer

The following diagram represents a fragment of the rhythmic material that appears for the first time shortly after the beginning of the movement. During the course of the excerpt this fragment is used in a number of different ways.

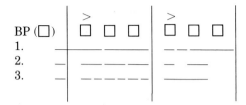

Q13   Which line in the diagram matches the fragment?
a. line 1
b. line 2
c. line 3

Q14   Considering the fragment in all its forms, how would you characterize its presence?
a. It is nearly always present.
b. It is absent for a considerable time.
c. It is present for only the first half of the excerpt.
d. It is contrasted with a less memorable pattern that is used nearly as often.

Invent a rhythmic pattern based on metric groups totaling 12 pulses. Memorize it. Play variations on the pattern. Invent a contrasting pattern. Build a rhythm composition using the original pattern, its variations, and the contrasting pattern.

OSTINATO

So far we have been exploring particular rhythmic patterns created by a composer for a specific composition. Such patterns are one aspect of what makes a given piece unique. The device known as the ostinato serves as a rhythmic backdrop in certain pieces of music. It is a rhythmic pattern—often fused with a melody—that *becomes* recognizable by being persistently repeated (more or less) throughout a given composition. Thus, though the pattern of any ostinato is often unique to the piece in which it occurs, its principle remains always the same—unity through repetition. We will examine two types of ostinato, historical dance rhythms and newly composed ostinatos.

Historical Dance Rhythms

Dance rhythms are a class of distinctive rhythmic patterns that exist independently of any particular piece and of any particular composer.

For obvious reasons the tempo, meter, and rhythmic patterns that accompany the steps of a specific dance tend to become more or less fixed. Any composer who wants to write a habanera, for example, would use one of the two rhythmic patterns that are characteristic of this traditional Cuban dance:

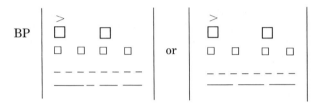

(Note that the second pattern groups the faster pulses in 3 + 3 + 2, a rhythmic effect found frequently in jazz.)

Example 5.6   Emmanuel Chabrier
              Habanera (excerpt)
              19th-century French composer

Example 5.7   Claude Debussy
              Preludes, Book 2, "La Puerta del Vino" (excerpt)
              19th/20th-century French composer

In comparing Examples 5.6 and 5.7, notice that Chabrier keeps the dance patterns to the fore, while Debussy keeps them subdued, suggesting rather than declaring their presence.

Many times, in concert music, a composer will keep the essence of a dance's rhythms, but will treat the basic pattern with considerable freedom. In such cases, the listener's familiarity with the basic pattern sets up expectations that the composer may or may not choose to fulfill; the composer thus creates the possibility of thwarted expectations— always a rich source of interest and tension. Listen to Examples 5.8–5.11 from this point of view.

Example 5.8   George Frideric Handel
              Keyboard Suite No. 11 D minor, Sarabande (Orchestral arrangement)
              18th-century German composer

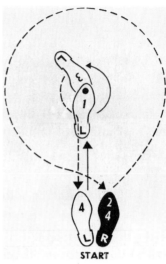

A sampler of dances and dancers. (Left: *Village Dancers,* c. 1650, by L. P. Boithard; below: *Children Dancing,* 1948, by Robert Gwathmey; above: *Fox Trot,* 1961, by Andy Warhol)

Example 5.9   Johann Sebastian Bach
Orchestral Suite No. 2, Sarabande
18th-century German composer

The sarabande is a rather dignified dance with a rhythmic pattern based on three slow pulses. In the first of these two sarabandes, Handel treats the pattern simply and straightforwardly; in the second, Bach's treatment is far freer and more elaborate.

Newly Composed Ostinatos

Using the same principles outlined earlier, composers may invent new ostinatos as the rhythmic basis of a section of a piece or as the basis of an entire composition. Ostinatos serve as an organizing device in the music of most cultures, functioning as a kind of accompaniment. Up to a certain point, repetition of an ostinato produces security and repose; beyond that point repetition tends to raise the level of tension by its very insistence. As an accompaniment, an ostinato affords another source of tension. Listen to the newly composed ostinato in Example 5.10.

Example 5.10   Terry Riley
A Rainbow in Curved Air (excerpt)
20th-century American composer

Here the ostinato competes for attention with the material being accompanied, and the listener must concentrate on both.

Examples 5.11–5.13 employ the characteristic rhythmic patterns, often repeated, of certain historical dances. Examples 5.14–5.16 are based on the repetition of a newly composed ostinato. Listen to each example and answer the accompanying question.

Example 5.11   Frédéric Chopin
Mazurka, Op. 33, No. 3
19th-century Polish composer

Q15   Within the basic three-pulse group is an implied pattern of short and long durations. Which pattern do you hear?
a. long—long—short
b. short—short—long
c. short—long—short

Pont des Arts, a bridge in Paris. Its repeating understructure functions somewhat as an ostinato does in music.

Example 5.12   Johann Sebastian Bach
            Orchestral Suite No. 3, Gavotte
            18th-century German composer

Q16   Which line in the diagram best matches the ostinato?

a. line 1
b. line 2
c. line 3

Example 5.13   Peter Ilich Tchaikovsky
Swan Lake, "Valse" (excerpt)
19th-century Russian composer

Q17   Where is the ostinato pattern in this historical dance rhythm
(waltz) found?
a. in the melody
b. in the accompaniment

Know

Example 5.14 Bill Chase
Paint It Sad
20th-century American composer

X Q18   Where is the ostinato found?
a. in the vocal part
b. in the guitar
c. in the drums
d. in the bass guitar

Know

Example 5.15   Carl Orff
Carmina Burana (excerpt)
20th-century German composer

Q19   Listen to the rhythm with the fastest pace. Does this ostinato
move consistently and without interruption or is it syncopated?
a. It moves consistently and without interruption.
b. It is syncopated.

Know

Example 5.16   *Salutation Song*
Traditional Indian music

Q20   How many ostinatos are heard?
a. one
b. two
c. three

Invent an ostinato pattern. In class or small groups try performing two or more ostinatos together, adding and dropping one at a time. Shape the piece by making things louder or softer. Make changes as needed to develop a piece that works well.

Compose a short percussion piece for three players, using as one element either a dance pattern or an ostinato. Try to build up some tension. Invent your own notation as needed.

Do some investigation of the relationship between music and dances. Try to find and listen to pieces with such dance titles as pavane, minuet, cakewalk, waltz, rumba, etc., and see how they compare with dictionary descriptions. Pick out a dance that interests you particularly and study it in some detail.

By now, it should be fairly obvious to you that creating and perceiving music can be a complicated affair. If you have been learning to listen closely and well, you will have gained some skill in coping with the complications discussed in this chapter: the intricacies of rhythm versus meter, of continuity versus contrast of rhythmic patterns, and the frequent tension in the conflict of these things as a composition unfolds. These listening skills will stand you in good stead as you increase and sharpen them in the chapters to come.

SYNTHESIS

Example 5.17 combines several of the topics of this chapter—unique rhythmic patterns, dance patterns, and ostinato—together with one aspect of music flowing freely in time (Chapter 3).

Example 5.17   Henry Purcell
Dido and Aeneas, "Thy Hand, Belinda" and "Dido's Lament"
17th-century English composer

RECITATIVE:

Thy hand, Belinda, darkness shades me,
On thy bosom let me rest.
More I would, but death invades me;
Death is now a welcome guest.

AIR:

When I am laid in earth,
May my wrongs create
No trouble in thy breast;
Remember me, but ah! forget my fate.

In the recitative, rhythm is a free-flowing response to the words, without the regularity of metric pulse groups, but the entire air is metrically organized, often with rhythmic patterns repeated.

Q21   Which words accompany this pattern:

    a. When I am laid in earth
    b. May my wrongs create
    c. But ah! forget my fate
    d. When I am laid, am laid in earth

Q22   A bit later, the following pattern emerges (with silences in the vocal line indicated by the blank spots in the diagram). What are the accompanying words?

    a. My wrongs create
    b. Remember me, remember me
    c. Remember me, but ah!
    d. Forget my fate, forget my fate

Q23   As the air begins, the orchestra commences an ostinato in the bass which has the following pitch contour and rhythm. How many times does this ostinato occur? (See pattern on p. 108.)

    a. twice
    b. six times
    c. eleven times

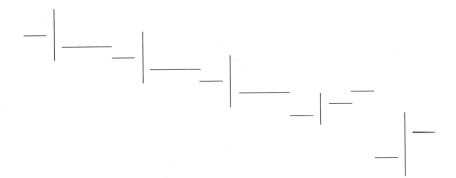

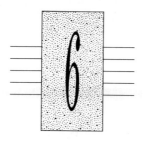

HOW
PITCH
FUNCTIONS

Music's domain is, of course, the sound space within which the human ear can hear, a spectrum usually described in terms of frequencies. As described in Chapter 1, *frequency* is the rate of to-and-fro vibration per second by a sounding body (such as a violin string, a drumhead, or the vocal cords). Remember that the slowest frequency the ear can hear is around 20 vibrations or cycles per second, and the fastest is around 18,000.* Below the audio range we hear separate pulses; above it are ultrasonic frequencies beyond the reach of the human ear. In Example 6.1, an oscillator of a synthesizer sweeps this entire spectrum.

---

*Frequencies are now usually expressed in units called *hertz* (abbreviated *Hz.*). One hertz is equal to one cycle per second; 20 Hz is thus the same frequency as 20 cycles per second, and 18 kHz is the same as 18,000 cycles per second.

Example 6.1   Synthesizer demonstration
of the audible frequency spectrum

Throughout this example sound is being generated. The break halfway through is the point at which the oscillator sweeps into the ultrasonic range and then returns.

As you listen to the frequencies generated by the synthesizer, your ears are responding to them as *pitches*. For reasons not entirely clear, though they go deep into our conditioning, we say that the slower the frequency, the "lower" the pitch; and the faster the frequency, the "higher" the pitch. We use this convention despite the fact that it has no physical validity. It would be physically accurate, however, to link frequency to length. Lower frequencies do have longer wave forms than higher frequencies. It is not common to speak of "long" or "short" pitches. Those terms are reserved for discussion about radio transmission (short wave or long wave).

THE PITCH CONTINUUM

Theoretically, the complete range of audible sound can be divided into an almost infinite number of pitches. You are now familiar enough with music to know that few pieces use them all. In most cases the actual number of different pitches used in a single composition is quite small. This chapter will deal with this much smaller number of pitches.

Played on a trumpet, the A above middle C produces a sound wave that "looks" like this.

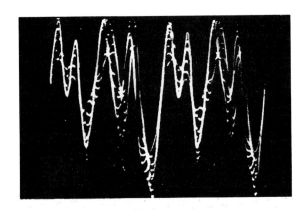

It has been said that pitch is one of the first elements a listener notices, but it is certainly not a universal truth. There are countless successful compositions that do not use distinguishable pitches. By distinguishable we mean a measurable, clearly distinct frequency that can be reproduced or imitated by another instrument. Some instruments do not produce such specific pitches. Just tap on a hard wood table and you will hear that you cannot sing any single pitch that matches the tap. Compositions that do not use distinct pitches use other elements, such as rhythm, to create their musical logic. Other chapters of this book offer excellent examples of that type of composition.

Music that uses distinct pitches can be divided into two broad categories: compositions in which one pitch dominates (a pitch hierarchy) and those that use pitch democratically (any pitch can vie for dominance). This chapter is restricted to the former: tonal music.

TONALITY

Tonality is created when one pitch becomes the focus of a composition. This focal pitch, called the *tonic*, is usually heard at the beginning and end of a piece. It is the pitch that all others defer to—from which all other pitches move away or progress toward. It is the musical center—the hub—of the piece.

Tonality is created in a number of ways:

1. The tonic pitch may be the starting point of a section or piece.
2. The tonic pitch may be the ending point of a section or piece.
3. It may be both.
4. It may simply be the most frequently heard pitch.

Here are three examples that will help you understand the concept. Sing the following songs (or have someone sing them for you). The T indicates the tonic pitch.

T   T
Joy to the world, the Lord is come!

This satisfies criterion 3: the tonic pitch is both the beginning and end of the line.

                             T
Let earth receive her king.

If this painting were a musical composition using a major or minor scale, which figure would be the tonic? (*The Last Supper*, c. 1498, by Leonardo da Vinci)

The second line satisfies criterion 2: the tonic pitch is the ending point.

Here is another example:

```
T  T        T
My country 'tis of thee,
                 T
Sweet land of liberty,
    T    T
Of thee I sing.
```

All four criteria are satisfied in this example.

> **Example 6.2**   Michael Kamen and Marty Fulterman
> *Beside You* (excerpt), 1970
> 20th-century American composers/performers

Through careful perception of this example we can learn a great deal about tonality. Tonality is created in great part by redundancy or repetition and the creation and resolution of expectation. Once we hear a tonic we expect the tonic to return again and again. If it returns too often, the repetition becomes boring. If it returns too infrequently, the strength of our expectation weakens. In the following number sequence, 1 is clearly the tonic number: 1 2 1 3 1 2 1 4 1 3 1 2 1. Its arrival is very predictable. Compare the first pattern to this one: 1 2 1 3 1 2 1 4 1 3 1 2 1 2 3 4 5 1 1. What happened? Is 1 still the tonic?

Listen to Example 6.2, a song you became familiar with in Chapter 2, several times. The song can be perceived in four different sections. Each of the four sections also can be divided into two parts.

Section one begins at the beginning of the song and ends with the word "began." It is also natural to hear this section as being in two parts, the first part ending on the word "stream." Do you hear the two parts?

The second section is very similar to the first. It begins with the word "I" and ends with "care." This section can also be divided into two parts with the break coming at the word "stare."

The third section is in complete contrast in regard to the pitches used in the first two. It begins "that I'd" and ends with the word "light." But again, like the two previous sections, this section can be divided into two parts at the word "night."

Finally, the song concludes with the phrase that begins "And peace . . . so quiet."

Before we examine the pitch material of the song, write out the complete lyric. There are some interesting poetic images that are fun to explore. Notice, for example, the reference to listening to a visual image.

The tonality of the song is very clearly established in the first section. The tonic pitch is heard on the second half of "river," on "the," "my," and at the end of "began."

Q1   How do the tonic pitches relate to the accented beats?
   a. They never fall on accented beats.
   b. They always fall on accented beats.
   c. They fall on accented and unaccented beats an equal number of times.
   d. They fall on accented beats most of the time.

Now listen to section two, the section most closely related to section one. The section ends on the word "care."

Q2   Does section two end on a tonic or non-tonic pitch?
   a. tonic
   b. non-tonic

Now listen to section three again. Pay particular attention to the words "night" and "light." Now compare these words with the last pitch in the example. The pitch is on the last part of "quiet."

Q3   The pitches on the three words in question are:
a. tonic on the first two and non-tonic on the last
b. tonic on all three
c. tonic on the last word only
d. tonic on the first two only

SCALES

Trying to explain the difference between red and orange to someone who has never seen color before is impossible. While colors have a specific vibrational frequency, the numbers cannot describe the colors. An easier but still difficult task would be to analyze the colors in a complicated painting. If we could name every color in the painting, we could organize and report the colors in relationship to their placement on the spectrum. Once the colors are placed in spectrum sequence we can recognize existing patterns. We can say, with certainty, "These are the colors used in this painting." But the spectrum is not the painting. It is merely a convenient way to report the use of color.

The scale is a convenient way of reporting the pitches present in a piece, whereby pitches are arranged in order from the lowest to highest. The word scale comes from the Italian word for ladder, *scala*. Like the rungs of a ladder, each successive pitch is higher than the previous one.

Most musical cultures select a certain number of scale models and therefore the task of matching scales is not completely impossible. Like a painting, however, the presentation of color or pitches in a sequence that moves from low to high may or may not have anything to do with the way the work flows. Paintings that are a literal, linear presentation of color might be just as boring as a composition made up solely of scales.

A history of scales is well beyond the scope of this book. Most scales were probably developed accidentally or by copying some observed phenomenon in nature. Within a culture the instrument builders may have had a lot to do with the development of scales. Once the holes are cut into a flute its degree of scale flexibility is fixed. The builder may have been trying to satisfy a theoretical hunch—history is full of examples of theory leading to adoption of a scale; also of the opposite: theory based on existing scales. It doesn't really matter.

What matters is the fact that different cultures get used to different scales and tend to judge other music by their "scale standard." In our culture, some people think of scales in terms of the piano. Because it was developed to play a certain set of scales, the piano cannot produce most scales in the world. Remember that a scale is the pitch material selected by the composer/performer. It can never be "wrong," only different.

Our own ears are conditioned, of course, by the major-minor scale system that has been central to Western music for several centuries. This system is only one of many that have developed in different regions at different periods in different cultures. Although various pitch systems (or scales) differ widely in number of pitches and in relationships between the pitches, none of them is inherently better than another, and all are potent sources of tension and repose in the shaping of music.

All scales have three things in common:

1. A selection of pitches within the pitch space of an octave (Example 6.3).
2. Established distances (or *intervals*) between the pitches in this octave span.
3. The tendency, within any piece, for one of its pitches to become the focus and final arrival point of all the other pitches—to become a *tonic*, as seen earlier.

Example 6.3   Synthesizer demonstration of octaves

All the sounds you hear in Example 6.3 are octaves, intervals that are characterized by their quality of "sound-alikeness," even though their actual pitches differ. This quality of *octave identity* is the basis for dividing up pitch space within any pitch system: every pitch is fixed in distance from every other pitch within the space of an octave; this pattern of fixed intervals then repeats from octave to octave through the available range.

Even if you don't play the piano, you can confirm the fact of octave identity for yourself at a keyboard. Look for the repeating pattern of black keys—two together, then three together. Go up and down the keyboard striking the left-hand key in each group of two black keys; you will be playing octaves and it will be evident to you that they are sound-alikes. To confirm the fact that pitches fixed at the same

We wouldn't know what time it was if any part of this clockwork failed to function properly in relation to every other part.

distance from each other within each octave form a repeating pattern, play the whole group of two-plus-three black keys from left to right at all the places it occurs. You will hear the sameness of each five-pitch group, as well as the octave identity of the corresponding pitches in each group.

The Pentatonic Scale

When you played the group of two-plus-three black keys, you were playing the basic five-pitch order of one of the oldest known pitch systems—the *pentatonic scale*.

Example 6.4   *Salutation* Song (excerpt)
Traditional Indian music

This song does not use all of the pitches of the pentatonic scale during the example. A selected number is used. You will easily recognize the primary importance of the lowest pitch as the point to which the other pitches constantly return. A pitch with this focal role is the *tonic*.

Q4 How many pitches are used?
   a. one
   b. two
   c. three
   d. four

Example 6.5 *Wild Geese Alighting on the Sandy Shores* (excerpt)
               Chinese music

This song also uses the pentatonic system, but it is more complex than Example 6.5 in two ways: more than one pitch seems to function as a tonic, and there are several occurrences of a pitch that does not fit into the pentatonic scale. This added pitch, which can be regarded as an auxiliary tone, creates tension because it is unexpected; it thus adds drama and intensity to the passage. Most pitch systems use auxiliary tones as tension-raisers.

Q5 Are the two instruments playing different pitch successions (melodies), or are they simply playing two versions of the same melody, one more elaborate than the other?
   a. two different melodies
   b. the exact same melody
   c. two different versions

The Major and Minor Scales

For over two centuries Western music has used a pitch system based on dividing the pitch space within an octave into twelve equidistant pitches. The interval between each of these pitches is called a *half-step*. At the keyboard, begin with the pitch C (see Figure 1) and move up or down to the nearest key, white or black. Continue in this way until you reach the C an octave above or below, and you will have played the twelve pitches most commonly used in Western music. You can establish the sound and feel of identity from octave to octave by continuing to play this key-to-next-key pattern between all the C's on the keyboard.

In playing this twelve-pitch scale you may think that the pitch relationships you hear don't have much in common with most of the tunes you know. The reason is that only seven of these twelve pitches, in a variety of scales, have been used traditionally as the actual basic pitch material of a given composition, with the other five pitches serving in different auxiliary ways. Two of the possible seven-pitch scales have been of primary importance in Western music for the last three hundred years. They are called the *major scale* and the *minor scale,* and they are both very familiar to your ears, whether or not you have ever heard their names. To hear the major scale, start with a C at the keyboard and play in succession all the white keys up or down through the next C. To hear the basic minor scale, do the same thing with the white keys A through A except for the key G; instead of G, play the black key just above it (G-sharp). In the major scale you played, C is the central pitch—the tonic; similarly, in the minor scale the tonic is A. To test just how strongly our ear needs to arrive at the tonic, try playing these two scales again, stopping on B for the C major scale and on G-sharp for the A minor scale. Do you find it possible to resist finally going on to the C and the A?

The major and minor scales sound quite different from each other because their interval structure—the distance from pitch to pitch—differs. Figure 2 shows that structure in half-steps (key-to-next-key, black or white) and whole-steps (two half-steps, of course). It should be evident that you could start these patterns on any one of the twelve pitches within the octave. If you did this you would be *transposing* to the scales of each of the twelve major and twelve minor "keys" used in much of our music. Each starting pitch becomes a new tonic, and wherever you start, the sound of "majorness" or "minorness" remains because the *relationship* between the pitches—their interval structure—is the same.

Figure 1

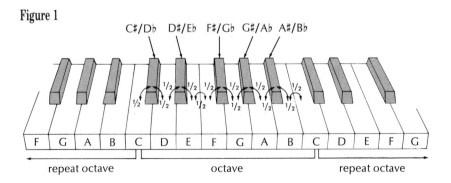

Figure 2

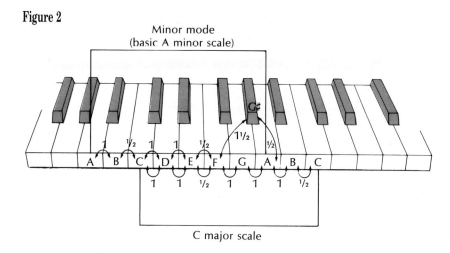

C major scale

Although major and minor scales are closely intertwined in a great many compositions, they can be made to function in a kind of contrast that creates a good deal of tension between the two. Example 6.6 illustrates this tension, as well as the difference in sound between the two scales.

Example 6.6   Franz Schubert
The Winter Journey, "Good Night" (excerpt)
19th-century Viennese composer

This verse of the song begins in minor, moves to major, and returns to minor. Here is the German text:*

> Was soll ich länger weilen, dass man mich trieb' hinaus?
> Lass irre Hunde heulen vor ihres Herren Haus!
> Die Liebe liebt das Wandern, Gott hat sie so gemacht,
> von Einem zu dem Andern, Gott hat sie so gemacht.
> Die Liebe liebt das Wandern, fein Liebchen, gute Nacht!
> von Einem zu dem Andern, fein Liebchen, gute Nacht!

*Translation: Why should I tarry longer, if I am to be rejected? Let mad dogs howl in front of their master's house! Love loves wandering, God has made it so. From one to the other, God has made it so. Love loves wandering, dear sweetheart, good night! From one to the other, dear sweetheart, good night!

Q6   Where does the change from minor to major occur?
   a. during line 2
   b. during line 3
   c. during line 4
   d. during line 5

Q7   Where does the change back to minor occur?
   a. during line 3
   b. during line 4
   c. during line 5
   d. during line 6

More Scales

While the major and minor scales have played the most prominent role in the past three hundred years of Western music, other scales with interval structures different from those of the major and minor prevailed during earlier centuries. To hear how the most important ones sound, you can go back to the keyboard and play *all white* keys as follows:

Scale	*White Keys*
Dorian	D through D
Phrygian	E through E
Lydian	F through F
Mixolydian	G through G

As with the major and minor scales, you can start a scale in any of these on any of the twelve available pitches, using black and white keys as necessary to preserve the relationships of half- and whole-steps. You should have no trouble in figuring out the pattern of half-steps and whole-steps of each scale.

After three centuries of little or no use, two of these scales, the Dorian and Mixolydian, have recently been incorporated with major and minor in a great deal of popular music, probably because of the influence of the blues.

Example 6.7   Lightnin' Hopkins
         Bad Luck and Trouble (excerpt)
         20th-century American performer/composer

The so-called blue notes (auxiliary tones) you can hear in this example modify the major scale so that it sounds somewhat Mixolydian or Dorian.

Choose a song you know well and try to play its melody on the piano, the guitar, or any other instrument.

Select six pitches at random within an octave and a half on any instrument. Arrange them in different ways (including repeating a pitch) to create interesting melodies. Which arrangements of pitches seem the most successful? Can you tell why?

Compose three melodies using the black keys of the piano. For each melody, establish a different pitch as the tonic center. How did you accomplish this?

Write another black-key melody that avoids any sense of a tonic center, organizing it mainly by a rhythmic pattern. How did you avoid creating a tonic?

THREE TONAL SYSTEMS

As you have just read and heard, the Western scale system is very complex. It is not, however, the most complex. There are other cultures, such as North and South Indian, with scales that are infinitely more complex and diverse. Whereas Western music basically uses seven scales, there are literally thousands of different scale combinations in these two Indian cultures. Other music, such as that from the Persian tradition, also has a more elaborate scale system than in the Western culture.

At the other extreme, music from Java, Indonesia, primarily uses only two scales. When you understand how pitch and tonality function within an elaborate yet closed tonal system within each of these three cultures you will understand why the great difference in the number of scales exists. Each culture's music is highly developed yet each generates musical complexity using different means:

1. Western music uses an elaborate system of chords that both accompany and have a life of their own. It is *harmonic* music.

2. Indian music relies on melodic intricacy to develop complex musical ideas. It is _linear_ music.
3. In Indonesian music performers simultaneously share a common scale but use no chords. The melodies they play are layered and interlocking; they generate a composite that is more complex than the sum of its parts. It could be called _stratified_ music.

The rest of this chapter explores each of the tonal systems.

HARMONIC MUSIC

Up to now our discussion of pitch systems has been in terms of _successions_ of pitches—and in many musical cultures a one-after-the-other succession is almost the only way pitches are ever used. Western music, however, has developed the _simultaneous combination_ of pitches extensively, ranging from the simplicity of just two pitches sounded together to the extreme density and complexity of the combinations you have heard in some of the earlier examples. In an introductory study, we can only discuss a few of the simplest simultaneous combinations (or chords) commonly used in the major and minor modes.

Triads and Seventh Chords

A _chord,_ theoretically speaking, is any set of three or more different pitches sounded simultaneously. In the major and minor scales, however, chords are built up by intervals of thirds (Figure 3).

At the keyboard, if you play the pitches C-E-G, F-A-C, or G-B-D simultaneously, you are playing _major triads_—chords with a major third on the bottom and a minor third on top. If you play the pitches D-F-A, E-G-B, or A-C-E, you are playing _minor triads_—with a minor third on the bottom and a major third on top. (Actually, any pitch of each of these chords can be the top or the bottom pitch without destroying the chord's identify. For example, try playing C-E-G, then E-G-C, then G-C-E.) Each of these triads may be extended by adding another third on top, making a _seventh chord:_ C-E-G-B (or B-flat), G-B-D-F (or F-sharp), D-F-A-C, etc.* Triads and seventh chords form the basic material of what is conventionally called _harmony._ We tend

---

*The term "seventh," like "second," "third," "fourth," "fifth," and "sixth," describes the interval formed by the bottom and top pitches.

Figure 3

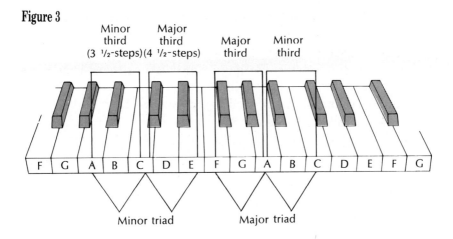

to think of these chords as agreeable sounds, in and of themselves, and you may want to experiment by building them on different pitches— seeing how they sound with now one pitch, now another above or below—or by duplicating a chord in more than one octave at a time.

Functional Relationships

The main point about chords, however, is not their structure, nor their separate identity, nor how well they may sound individually, but how they function in relationship to each other—that is, what their role is as an organizing power in a composition, and as a means of raising or lowering the level of tension. To discuss function in even the most basic way we need a little more terminology: the names and numbers conventionally used to identify the chords in a mode. To keep things simple, we will stay in the major mode and the C major scale:

C	D	E	F	G	A	B
tonic	supertonic	mediant	subdominant	dominant	submediant	leading tone
I	II	III	IV	V	VI	VII

The most important chord is the tonic (I). Once established, it is the focal point, the goal of motion, the center of repose. Any move away from the tonic raises tension—an expectation of return to it. In fact, the whole edifice of functional relationships between chords is an intricate network of expectations: what chord will follow what chord on the way home to the tonic. For any listener who is tuned in to these expectations there is a never-ending flow of tension-repose effects as expectations are raised, fulfilled, delayed, or denied.

The next most important chord is the dominant (V). Its function is to introduce the tonic, and these two chords alone can establish the tonal base or center—the key.

Example 6.8   A. P. Carter
              Jimmy Brown the Newsboy (excerpt)
              20th-century American composers

The first verse, after the instrumental introduction, begins with the tonic, changes to the dominant on the word "Brown" and back to the tonic on "town."

Q8   On what words do the changes takes place in the second verse?
      a. town / brown
      b. street / feet
      c. star / head

Q9   Does the pattern continue in the same way or does it change?
      a. It remains the same.
      b. It changes.

A third chord, the subdominant (IV), is joined with tonic and dominant in many well-known tunes. Sometimes it moves directly to the tonic, sometimes it introduces the dominant on the way to the tonic, and sometimes it interrupts the direct motion of dominant to tonic.

Example 6.9   Johnny Winter
              Rock and Roll (excerpt)
              20th-century American composer/performer

This piece begins with an instrumental introduction on the tonic chord only, firmly establishing it as the center. The rest of the excerpt consists of two verses of the song. Each verse has the chord structure outlined in the following diagram, which shows how long each chord lasts in terms of the two-pulse basic meter. The tempo is slow.

I ──
| □ □ | □ □ | □ □ | □ □ | □ □ | □ □ | □ □ | □ □ |

IV───────────────────────────
| □ □ | □ □ | □ □ | □ □ |

I ─────────────────────────
| □ □ | □ □ | □ □ | □ □ |

V──────────────
| □ □ | □ □ |

IV──────────────
| □ □ | □ □ |

I ─────────────────────
| □ □ | □ □ | □ □ | □ □ |

In the fifth line of the diagram the subdominant (IV) chord interrupts the expected direct succession of V to I, thus introducing a brief moment of tension. During the second verse there is less tension at this point because the surprise has already been heard.

Q10   On what words of the text in verses 1 and 2 does this chord
       change take place?
       a. There'll be / Gonna be
       b. Gonna be / Rock'n
       c. Mama / There'll be

Following are lines from three familiar songs. On what words do the chords change? (More than one answer may be correct.)

Q11   Mary had a little lamb, little lamb, little lamb
       a. first "little lamb"
       b. second "little lamb"
       c. third "little lamb"

Q12   Silent night, holy night, all is calm, all is bright
       a. Silent night / all is calm
       b. Holy night / all is bright
       c. All is calm / all is bright

Q13   Old MacDonald had a farm, ee-i-ee-i-o
       a. MacDonald
       b. farm
       c. a
       d. ee-i-ee-i-o

Example 6.10   Frédéric Chopin
               Prelude, Op. 28. No. 7
               19th-century Polish composer

In Example 6.10 we noted the brief interruption of the expected V-I
chord progression. In this piece there is a somewhat more dramatic
harmonic happening. As shown in the diagram, a regular alternation of dominant-to-tonic is interrupted by an unexpected appearance of the VI chord. The tension thus raised is gently lowered by
a commonly used succession of VI-II-V-I.

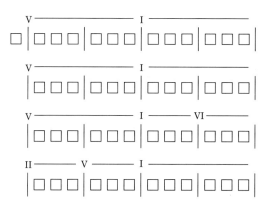

Example 6.11   W. A. Morris and Z. Morris
               Salty Dog (excerpt)
               20th-century American composers

The chord succession at the end of Example 6.10 is one used in a
great many older pieces. In *Salty Dog,* we hear it in especially
compressed and repetitive fashion. The diagram again shows the
chords heard on the pulses of the two-pulse basic meter, in a rather
fast tempo. (The signs ‖: and :‖ at beginning and end indicate that
everything between is repeated, in this case each successive verse.)

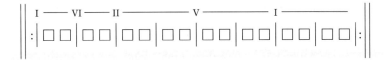

In this sequence each chord from VI on has the feel of introducing the next, and there is, in fact, a kind of dominant-to-tonic relationship between VI and II and II and V, as well as between the real V and I.

Q14   Does the chord succession change or stay the same during the instrumental sections?
a. It changes.
b. It remains the same.

Your ear has probably told you by now that these simple chord relationships are like many you hear in a wide range of music. Once having grasped the idea of the *function* of chords, you will have a basis for distinguishing between the expected and the unexpected, and for sensing the power of chord succession in both raising and resolving tension.

Devise a sequence of chords that pleases you. After you learn it well, add a melody to the chords. Play the piece on your instrument, or ask a friend to play the chords or melody with you.

LINEAR MUSIC

There is a great deal of music in the world that is purely linear. The harmony that developed in Western Europe (and that now has spread throughout the world) is a fairly new invention. Before the seventeenth century music in the West—and everyplace else—was primarily linear. Chords did not exist. More than one melody could be presented at the same time, but the emphasis was on the melodic line.

North Indian classical music, our representation for all linear musics, is both purely linear and highly developed.

The Raga System

Most Indian music is improvised. The improvisation is not random or arbitrary. Improvisations are developed from *ragas,* traditional melodic patterns designed to evoke a mood, feeling, or the essence of a defined experience (such as specific time of the day, season, or climatic phenomenon). While several thousand ragas are theoretically possible, modern musicians seem to favor seventy or eighty.

Ragas are not scales but are derived from a set of ten parent *thats* (scale forms). The *thats* (pronounced *thoughts*) are presented below. For purposes of discussion the steps of each *that* are expressed as whole- or half-steps so they can be related to the intervals of the piano. Whereas Western musicians use numbers or Italian syllables (Do, Re, Mi, Fa, Sol, La, Ti, Do) to indicate scale positions, the Indians use the syllables Sa, Re, Ga, Ma, Pa, Dha, Ni, Ṡa. Here are the three systems shown together:

1	2	3	4	5	6	7	1
Do	Re	Mi	Fa	Sol	La	Ti	Do
Sa	Re	Ga	Ma	Pa	Dha	Ni	Ṡa

The Thats

Bilaval

	1		1		1/2		1		1		1		1/2	
Sa		Re		Ga		Ma		Pa		Dha		Ni		Ṡa*

†Kalyan

	1		1		1		1/2		1		1		1	
Sa		Re		Ga		Ma'		Pa		Dha		Ni		Ṡa

†Khamaj

	1		1		1/2		1		1		1/2		1	
Sa		Re		Ga		Ma		Pa		Dha		N̲i		Ṡa

Asawari

	1		1/2		1		1		1/2		1		1	
S		R		G̲		M		P		D̲		N̲		Ṡ

*A dot over a syllable indicates the higher octave; a dot below indicates the lower octave.
†The Indians use two symbols to indicate a lowering or raising of a pitch by one half-step. The tivra (') raises the pitch by approximately one half-step and the Komal (‿) lowers the pitch by the same amount.

Bhairav

	1/2		1 1/2		1/2		1		1/2		1 1/2		1/2	
S		R̲		G		M	P		D̲		N		Ṡ

Bhairavi

	1/2		1		1		1		1/2		1		1	
S		R̲	G̲		M	P		D̲		N̲		Ṡ

Kafi

	1		1/2		1		1		1		1/2		1	
S		R		G̲		M	P		D		N̲		Ṡ

Marwa

	1/2		1 1/2		1		1/2		1		1		1/2	
S		R̲		G	M'		P		D		N		Ṡ

Purvi

	1/2		1 1/2		1		1/2		1/2		1 1/2		1/2	
S		R̲		G	M'		P		D̲		N		Ṡ

Todi

	1/2		1		1 1/2		1/2		1/2		1 1/2		1/2	
S		R̲	G		M'		P		D̲1		N		Ṡ

On the surface, the *thats* look like the Western scales described earlier.
If you were to play these on the piano, you would hear the following
rough equivalents:

Aswari	minor
Bhairav	none
Bhairavi	Phrygian
Bivaval	major
Kafi	Dorian
Kalyan	Lydian
Khamaj	Mixolydian
Marwa	none
Purvi	none
Todi	none

Why can't these *thats* be duplicated on the piano? The piano has 12
fixed pitches between Do and Do, the octave. In Indian music there are
22 possible pitches between Sa and Ṡa. Sa and Pa are never changed
but Re, Ga, Ma, Dha, and Ni have a variety of positions. There are two
pitch positions between S and R: S R̲ R. (Every line added indicates a
lowering of the basic pitch.) There are three pitches between Ga and
Ma:G M̳ M̲ M. This is possible because most Indian instruments can

slide from one pitch to the other either by covering more or less of the tone holes on the aerophones or stretching (bending) strings. Of course, a voice can reproduce thousands of gradations within the octave. These very fine distinctions may be difficult for the inexperienced listener to hear but they are an important expressive ingredient to the experienced listener.

In Example 6.12, Ravi Shankar, one of India's great musicians, will sing *That Kalyan*.

Example 6.12   Ravi Shankar
                That Kalyan
                Classical Indian music

Did you notice that Shankar ornamented nearly every syllable? This is an important characteristic of Indian music. It is the exception to attack a pitch directly. The line is always ornamented.

Given the fact there are only ten parent scales, how can there be thousands of ragas? The best way to answer that question is to closely examine one specific raga.

Raga Yaman

Raga Yaman is derived from *That Kalyan*. Kalyan consists of seven pitches ascending and seven pitches descending:

S R G M' P D N Ṡ | Ṡ N D P M' G R S

It is common for ragas to have a different number of pitches in the ascending form of the scale than in the descending form. These are the possibilities.

ascending	descending
5	5
5	6
5	7
6	5
6	6
6	7
7	5
7	6
7	7

Raya Yaman is constructed as a six-pitch scale ascending—
R G M' D N Ṡ—and seven descending—
Ṡ N Ḍ P M' G R S.

A raga is more than a series of pitches. *Yaman* has very strict rules that underlie improvisation. A few of them follow:

1. Sa may not ascend to Re; Ma' may ascend to Dha but not to Pa.
2. Ni and Ga are important pitches that often serve as the focal points for improvisation.

In addition to the above rules, several phrases are traditionally heard in *Yaman*. Here are a few:

1. Ṇ R S
2. G R G R S
3. P M' G P R S

You can see now that each *that* can generate numerous ragas. The possibilities expand enormously when one additional variable is added: a raga may borrow scale materials from more than one *that*.

Remember the rules for *Yaman:*

1. Sa may not ascend to Re.
2. Ma' may ascend to Dha but not to Pa.
3. Ni and Ga are important pitches.
4. Ṇ R S is important.
5. G R G R S is important.
6. P M' G P R S is important.

Q15   Compare the relative importance of Ga and Ni in the following example.
   a. Ga is more important in this example.
   b. Ni is more important.
   c. They are of equal importance.

Q16   Which subsection contains the gesture Ṇ R S?
   a. Section a
   b. Section d
   c. Section e
   d. Section g

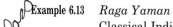 **Example 6.13**   *Raga Yaman*
                    Classical Indian music (excerpt)

This example of *Raga Yaman* will demonstrate one artist's approach to this raga. This is a recording of a live concert. In addition to the solo bansuri (flute) you will hear a second accompanying bansuri. The second bansuri is merely supportive (an Indian tradition) and not notated below. Two drones are also heard. One is electronic and the other played on the tamboura, an Indian chordophone. The drones play Sa and Pa exclusively. Only the principal pitches are shown.

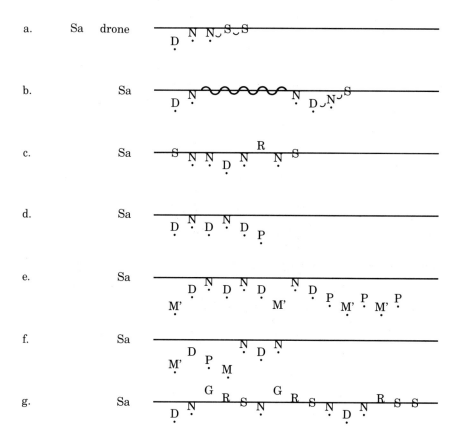

This improvisation reveals another important characteristic of Indian ragas. Note that the performer concentrates his efforts on the pitches below Sa, which are the lowest pitches that can be played on this particular bansuri. If we were to listen to the entire improvisation (more than thirty minutes) we would discover that the artist moves slowly upward until the entire raga has been "revealed." In subsection seven he begins to move toward Ga. The artistry of the raga performer is judged, in part, by the creativity he or she demonstrates in this process of revelation.

STRATIFIED MUSIC

Stratified music is best thought of as a series of layers, or strata, stacked one on top of the other. Each stratum is an elaboration of a single, slow-moving melody. It is as if a melody and a series of variations of that melody were played at the same time. In visual terms, one could imagine a series of transparent images, each a different color and more elaborate than the original image, stacked together so you can see each image individually or as a complex

A bansuri player.

composite. For example, the A printed below is shown as a separate stratum and as a composite:

$$A + Ā + A + A = Ā$$

Our model for stratified music comes from the island of Java in Indonesia. The music we will hear is performed by a gamelan. You heard the gamelan earlier in Example 3.12. You will recall that it consists primarily of idiophones (gongs, metal kettles, and metal and wooden xylophones), vocalists, membranophones (small and large drums), and a bowed chordophone (the rebab). The example you will hear later consists only of idiophones and membranophones.

Javanese Scales

The music of Java uses two parent scales, *slendro* and *pelog*, each of which has three different modes, which are determined by melodic tendencies and the importance of specific pitches. The pitches of slendro are distinctly different from those of pelog and cannot be reproduced on the same idiophones. The Javanese musicians actually play different instruments (idiophones) for each of these two scales.

Pelog, used in Example 6.14, is a five- or six-pitch scale selected from seven tuned bars of the idiophone. The bars are tuned perfectly but do not match any Western scale. There has been no attempt to tune the bars to Western scales. Why should there be? In fact, every gamelan is tuned differently, according to the wishes of the performers who use the instruments.

Three modes of Pelog are:

1. Nem: Pitches 1, 2, 3, 5, and 6 with a rare use of 4. Pitches 1, 2, and 3 are important and are heard in the normal pitch position on register.
2. Lima: Pitches 1, 2, 3, 5, 6 and rarely 4. Pitches 1 and 5 are important and are heard in the low register.
3. Barang: Pitches 2, 3, 5, 6, 7 and rarely 4.

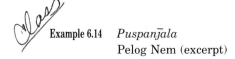

Example 6.14   *Puspañjala*
Pelog Nem (excerpt)

The central metaphor in Javanese music is the circle; the music is constructed as a series of repeated cycles. The pitch that starts a cycle also ends it. The cycle for Puspañjala is 16 slow pulses. The beginning and ending pitches are accompanied by a very low gong.

Listen to Example 6.14a several times. It is important for you to become familiar with this melody. The Javanese call it the *nuclear theme* because it is the nucleus of the entire composition. All other strata are derived from this theme. The nuclear theme is played by three metal xylophones: the slenthem, demung, and saron/barung. Follow the theme as you listen. (The circles indicate gong tones.)

pulse	16	1 2 3 4 5 6 7 8 9 10 11 12 13 14 15	16
nuclear theme	⑥	3 2 1 6 3 5 3 2 5 3 2 1 3 2 1	⑥
	gong		gong

Note the importance of 3, 2, 1 in this melody. Remember, this is one of the characteristics of Pelog Nem.

Example 6.14b demonstrates the nuclear theme joined by the first-elaboration theme, played by the saron panerus, a different xylophone. The saron panerus plays four pitches in the time of each nuclear pitch.

pulse	16		1		2		3		4		5	
nuclear theme	⑥		3		2		1		6		3	
saron penerus	6	6 3 3	2	2 3 3	2	2 1 1	6	6 1 1	6	6 3 3	5	5 3 3
	gong											

pulse	6		7		8		9		10		11	
nuclear theme	5		3		2		5		3		2	
saron penerus	5	5 3 3	2	2 3 3	2	2 5 5	3	3 5 5	3	3 2 2	1	1 2 2

pulse	12		13		14		15		16	
nuclear theme	1		3		2		1		⑥	
saron penerus	1	1 3 3	2	2 3 3	2	2 1 1	3	6 1 1	6	
									gong	

Q17   How would you describe the relationship between 6.14a and
6.14b?
a. There is no pattern of variation.
b. The pattern is created by first playing the next pitch of the
nuclear theme twice and then playing the principal pitch twice.
c. The pattern is created by first playing the principal pitch twice
and then playing the next pitch of the nuclear theme twice.
d. A combination of b and c.

Example 6.14c superimposes a different melody on the nuclear
theme. This melody is played by the gambang, a wooden xylophone, one octave lower.

The gambang melody has eight pitches to each pitch of the
nuclear theme.

pulse	16	1	2
nuclear theme	⑥	3	2
gambang	6 6 1 6 1 2 3 2	3 2 1 2 6 1 2 1	2 2 1 3 2 1 6 5

pulse	3	4	5
nuclear theme	1	5	3
gambang	3 3 3 3 5 6 3 5	6 6 1 6 1 2 3 2	3 3 1 3 2 1 2 1

pulse	6	7	8
nuclear theme	5	3	2
gambang	6 6 1 6 1 2 1 2	3 1 2 6 1 2 6 1	2 6 1 6 1 2 3 2

pulse	9	10	11
nuclear theme	5	3	2
gambang	3 2 1 6 1 6 1 2	3 2 1 6 5 3 3 3	3 3 3 3 5 6 5 6

pulse	12	13	14
nuclear theme	1	3	2
gambang	1 6 1 6 1 2 3 2	3 2 1 2 6 1 2 1	2 2 1 3 2 1 6 5

pulse	15	16	
nuclear theme	1	⑥	
gambang	3 3 3 3 5 6 3 5	6	
		gong	

Can you find patterns in the elaboration? Compare the first pitch
of each eight pitch grouping with the principal pitch. What other
patterns emerge?

In 6.14d we hear a new instrument: the bonang barung. This is an instrument made up of inverted kettles. The elaboration played by the bonang barung is at the same speed as the saron penerus, with four subdivisions of each pulse. This elaboration frequently incorporates empty subdivisions (silence), notated with a dash (—).

pulse	16				1				2				3				4				5		
nuclear theme	⑥				3				2				1				6				3		
bonang barung	6	3	2	3	—	3	2	3	2	1	6	1	—	1	6	1	6	3	5	3	—	3 5 3

pulse	6				7				8				9				10				11		
nuclear theme	5				3				2				5				3				2		
bonang barung	5	3	2	3	3	2	3	2	5	3	5	—	5	3	5	3	2	1	2	—	2 1 2		

pulse	12				13				14				15				16		
nuclear theme	1				3				2				①				⑥		
bonang barung	1	3	2	3	—	3	2	3	2	1	6	1	—	1	6	1	6		

Q18 How does the pattern of silences develop?
   a. There is no pattern.
   b. After an irregular pattern there is an alternation (at principal pitches) of a unison pitch and a silence.
   c. The pattern is regular.

Q19. What is the pattern of elaboration?
   a. The elaboration is always based on the principal pitch and the next pitch in the nuclear theme.
   b. The elaboration is always based on the principal pitch and two pitches forward.
   c. The elaboration is based on the principal pitch and the previous pitch.
   d. The elaboration is based on the principal pitch and/or the next or next two pitches of the nuclear theme.

Example 6.14e is our final demonstration of elaboration. We now hear the bonang penerus, a second set of inverted kettles. The bonang penerus divides each pulse into eight subdivisions but adds periodic moments of silence as in the previous example. This elaboration is really a variation of Example 6.14d. Listen to it several times. You should be able to follow the nuclear theme and this elaboration at the same time.

pulse	16	1	2
nuclear theme	⑥	3	2
bonang penerus	6 3 2 3 — 3 2 3 — 3 2 3 — 3 2 3 2 1 6 1 — 1 6 1		

pulse	3	4	5
nuclear theme	1	6	3
bonang penerus	— 1 6 1 — 1 6 1 6 3 5 3 — 3 5 3 — 3 5 3 — 3 5 3		

pulse	6	7	8
nuclear theme	5	3	2
bonang penerus	5 3 2 3 — 3 2 3 — 3 2 3 — 3 2 3 2 5 3 5 — 5 3 5		

pulse	9	10	11
nuclear theme	5	3	2
bonang penerus	— 5 3 5 — 5 3 5 3 2 1 2 — 2 1 2 — 2 1 2 — 2 1 2		

pulse	12	13	14
nuclear theme	1	3	2
bonang penerus	1 3 2 3 — 3 2 3 — 3 2 3 — 3 2 3 2 1 6 1 — 1 6 1		

pulse	15
nuclear theme	1
bonang penerus	— 1 6 1 — 1 6 1

Example 6.14f combines all of the above elements and adds several more, as follows:

1. Gender barung—a metal xylophone playing four pulses to each principal pitch (occasionally, two pitches are played at the same time).
2. Kendang—a set of hand drums playing an accompanying part (they are the actual leader of the group).
3. Ketuk and kempyang—small kettles used as time keepers; they alternate.
4. Kempul—a gong on pulse 12.
5. Kenong—a set of large tuned kettles that play pitch 2 (on pulse 8) and pitch 6 (on pulse 16).

Now listen to the entire 16-pulse cycle with all of the instruments at least four times.

1. Follow the nuclear theme and notice the elaborations.
2. Follow one elaboration and notice the other elaborations.
3. Let your focus shift from line to line.
4. Try to hear it all at the same time.

FOREGROUND
AND
BACKGROUND

Most of the music we listen to is complex, with more than one thing usually vying for our attention at any one time. This is so generally true that listening to a work like Example 7.1 is a startling revelation of just how much interest there can be in a single-line *(monophonic)* piece, and what a great range of expressive qualities is possible.

Example 7.1 *Ginryu Koku* (excerpt)
Traditional Japanese music

With no competition from other instruments, this player of the shakuhachi, an end-blown vertical flute of bamboo, explores its full possibilities—every shade of loudness, pitch, range, and tone color.

A shakuhachi, the Japanese flute you hear in Example 7.1.

Q1   In this example, the performer uses gradual dynamic changes to create the illusion of the music advancing and receding. How are the dynamic changes applied?
  a. They change in a sudden, immediate manner.
  b. They change very gradually, over five or six notes.
  c. They change very gradually, commonly on one note.

Q2   How is vibrato used by the performer?
  a. constantly, throughout the example
  b. variably, with many shadings
  c. Vibrato is not used in this example.

Improvise some single-line melodies on the piano or any other instrument. Exploit changes in loudness, range, and, if possible, tone color. If you use a piano, try different pressures on the keys. You might depress the damper pedal (the one on the right), then pluck the strings with a pick, fingernail, paper clip, or some other handy device.

Single-line music is an infrequent part of our experience. More commonly, we face the problem of which of several things to listen to. In a song, for instance, shall we concentrate on the singer's line and words, the pianist playing chords, the bass with a line of its own, or the rhythmic support of the drums? If we ignore everything but the vocal line, we may be missing interesting things in the other parts. Learning to concentrate on each of the parts, then on their relationship to each other, and, finally, taking in everything at once may mean many listenings, but the reward of enriched experience makes the effort well worthwhile. One way to begin is to pay simultaneous attention to a obvious musical foreground and a less obvious background.

MUSICAL FOREGROUND

Single Dominance

To say that a musical element is in the foreground is to say that it dominates its surroundings by being heard more prominently than anything else. It can dominate in many ways: by being loudest, by

In terms of dominance, there is no competiton for our attention here. The painting is foreground alone, and we are conscious of nothing but the head. (*Senecio,* 1922, by Paul Klee)

being the most active line in rhythm or pitch, by being lowest or highest, or by being distinctly different in sound. Simply put, any musical idea will dominate if it is the most evident or most interesting thing going on at the moment. Examples 7.2–7.5 explore some of the characteristics of musical dominance.

Example 7.2   Johann Sebastian Bach
Cantata No. 140, "Sleepers Awake"
Chorale, "Zion Hears the Watchman Calling" (excerpt)
18th-century German composer

There are three independent lines in this excerpt—the high strings, the low strings, and the unison tenors. During the first section only the high and low strings are heard, with the former clearly dominant; they are louder, more active, and altogether more interesting. The lower line has its own interest, as you will note if you focus on it, but the top line commands more attention. When the tenors enter in the second section, try paying attention to each line in turn.

Q3   Which of the three lines dominates in the second section?
 a. the high strings
 b. the low strings
 c. the unison tenor line

Q4   What is it that raises the level of tension at this point?
 a. the significant change in the basic pulse
 b. the extreme pitch variation in the tenor line
 c. the necessity of concentrating on two independent lines

Example 7.3   Michael Kamen and Marty Fulterman
     Beside You (excerpt)
     20th-century American composers/performers

[handwritten: homophonic   singer – melody]

This excerpt is for vocalist, guitar, oboes, and cello. Although the guitar part is more active, in both rhythm and melody, you will probably find that the human voice, carrying the main melody and the words, is almost irresistibly dominant, as it is in most songs.

Q5   Listen to the relationship between the oboes and guitar. How do their relative paces compare?
 a. They move at the same pace.
 b. The oboes are slower than the guitar.
 c. The guitar is slower than the oboes.

Q6   Listen to the guitar part in relation to the voice. Why can the guitar's pace be considered both faster and slower than the pace of the voice?
 a. because the pace of the voice part is variable
 b. because the guitar part includes a bass line that moves at a different, slower pace level

Q7   At one point in the song the accompaniment comes to a brief pause creating a dramatic effect on a particular word. Which word is it?
 a. peace
 b. beside
 c. sunrise
 d. quiet

Example 7.4   Darius Milhaud
     The Creation of the Earth (excerpt)
     20th-century French composer

[handwritten: say   most predominant]

GENERAL GEORGE WASHINGTON.
Reviewing the Western army at Fort Cumberland the 18ᵗʰ of Octobᵣ 1794,

Although there is plenty of detail in the background, the foreground figure of General Washington is clearly dominant. (*General George Washington,* c. 1794, by Frederick Kemmelmeyer)

This work is written for a chamber (small) orchestra that includes percussion and saxophone. The excerpt opens with strings and piano playing undulating figures at a fast meter level, while the saxophone plays a smooth, sustained melody with timpani punctuating lightly. This group is joined by trumpets and, later, trombones, culminating in a climax. The saxophone dominates for two reasons: it has the principal melody and its tone color is very distinctive. Although the piano and strings are more active, their sameness of material and motion tends to make them recede in interest.

Q8   How does the pace of the saxophone compare with that of the piano and strings?

a. The saxophone is slower.

b. The saxophone is faster.

c. They move at the same pace.

Q9   Which statement best explains why our attention is drawn to the
saxophone in this example?
  a. The saxophone is noticeably louder than the other parts.
  b. The saxophone part has a wide range of dynamic changes.
  c. The saxophone part has the most melodic interest.

Shifting Dominance

Theoretically, the number of instruments and voices that can be
combined in any composition is unlimited, but when the ear is
presented with more than it can take in, as may well be the case in the
Example you are about to hear, it tends to filter out what it can't
assimilate and to focus on what surfaces as foreground material. Even
in much less dense music there may be two or more distinct lines
combined in such a sustained way as to require the ear to bounce
around from one part to another, trying to pick up enough of each to
absorb the full context. Such music has traditionally been called
polyphonic. Several relationships between its lines are possible:

1. More than one line has independent interest, but one line
   clearly dominates.
2. All lines are relatively equal and clearly perceivable,
   eliminating any foreground-background conflict of interest.
3. Interest shifts as one line then another dominates in an
   exchange of foreground-background roles.
4. No clear pattern develops, due to the extreme density of
   events.

Example 7.5   Peter Ilich Tchaikovsky
              1812 Overture (excerpt)
              19th-century Russian composer

This excerpt begins with a great deal of activity, as various
ideas compete for attention in constantly shifting foreground-
background relationships, eventually reaching a peak of conflict.
Suddenly there is but a single melody, powerfully reinforced in
various octaves by strings and winds. After this passage finally
winds down, the outburst of competing sounds and ideas reaches
an even greater climax than before. The single-line passage, which
functions as a link between what precedes and follows it, attains
its dramatic effect largely by contrast with what has come before:

after the tumult of competing ideas, the stark singularity of only one thing to listen to—foreground alone.

Examples 7.6–7.9 are further examples of shifting dominance.

Example 7.6   Franz Schubert
The Little Village (Dörfchen) (excerpt)   *rhythmic unison*
19th-century Viennese composer

homophonic

There are four voice parts in this piece, all moving together in rhythmic unison.

Q10   Which voice part emerges as the dominating one? Why?
   a. All parts are heard equally.
   b. The top voice part, because it has the principal melody.
   c. The bottom voice part, because it provides the bass line.
   d. The guitar accompaniment, because it provides a different color.

Example 7.7   George Frideric Handel
Samson, "Let the Bright Seraphim" (excerpt)
18th-century German composer

Clearly, the two melodic lines of this piece are independently interesting in their exchange of musical ideas, one line repeating what the other has just played. This technique is called *imitation*. At times one line dominates, but then the exchange takes place and the roles reverse. Sometimes, the two lines are identical in interest.

And occasionally in music from this stylistic period, ornamentation (an embellishment of the original melody) is added to the imitation.

Q11   In this example, which part is being imitated?
   a. The soprano is being imitated by the trumpet.
   b. The trumpet is being imitated by the soprano.

Example 7.8   *Song to Drive Birds into a Trap*
Music of Chad

The two boys sing the same series of melodic formulas, but in different order. Though the microphone placement for this recording and differences in voice quality may make one line seem to dominate, the two parts are of equal interest, and, at any given moment, highly independent of each other.

Q12   How would you characterize the foreground-background
      relationship of this example?
      a. two independent lines with one line dominating
      b. two relatively equal lines
      c. two lines exchanging domination in foreground-background
         roles
      d. no clear pattern because of the extreme density of events

There are so many delightful things going on in this sixteenth-century Persian
miniature that it is hard to know where to look first. It even has two names, *The
Eavesdropper* and *The Bathers*.

Example 7.9   Györy Ligeti
               Atmosphères (excerpt)
               20th-century Hungarian composer

Atmosphères challenges the listener to experience the interesting juxtaposition of a series of complicated, yet highly independent events. As the composition begins to unfold, try to determine if any recurring relationship of background-foreground roles develops.

Q13   How would you characterize the foreground-background relationship of this example?
       a. two independent lines with one line dominating
       b. two relatively equal lines
       c. two lines exchanging domination in foreground-background roles
       d. no clear pattern because of the extreme density of events

Get together with two or three friends and, using instruments such as drums, water glasses, saucers, etc., invent a composition with sections that have different foreground-background relationships: a single line dominant, two lines dominant and one supporting, all lines equal. If you use your imagination and stick with it, you will probably make a piece that pleases you.

Listen to one of your favorite pieces and try to observe more foreground-background relationships than you ever noticed before.

Look at some nonrepresentational paintings, studying their foreground-background properties.

MUSICAL BACKGROUND

So far we have concentrated on the foreground of two kinds of pieces: those in which a single line dominates, with or without accompaniment, and those with shifting foreground relationships. Now we will turn to the background (or accompaniment) of works in which one line is clearly dominant.

The accompaniment's framework and support for the dominant line can consist of nothing but rhythm, as with drum patterns, or it may be mostly a matter of pitch, often organized as chords. Sometimes

Can you keep your attention fixed on the looming cypress in the foreground, or are you irresistibly drawn to the turbulence of the background sky? (*The Starry Night,* 1889, by Vincent Van Gogh. Collection, the Museum of Modern Art, New York.)

rhythm and pitch operate together to form a unified accompaniment, as in Example 7.10.

> Example 7.10   Woody Guthrie
> *John Henry*
> 20th-century American composer/performer

Many times, however, rhythm and pitch are more independent of each other, and it is worth examining them separately in some detail.

The Rhythmic Factor

The most obvious function of rhythm in an accompaniment is to provide a time frame for the dominant material, usually by reinforcing the basic meter while adding activity at other meter levels. Sometimes the interplay of rhythmic patterns is so interesting that it competes with the dominating line. When this happens the accompaniment becomes a source of tension, as we get involved with both accompaniment and melody and try to cope with their combined interest. Rhythmic accompaniment can strongly influence mood or atmosphere by regulating the flow of musical energy (as it did in Example 7.3, for instance).

Examples 7.11 and 7.12 illustrate some of the kinds of interest a rhythmic accompaniment can generate. In Example 7.12 pitch is also a factor, but our attention will be on rhythm.

Example 7.11   Traditional music from North Africa
                Music for a Camel Tournament (excerpt)

The solo voice enters a split second before the rhythm begins. The time is kept by a steady rhythm provided by hand clappers and a hand drum. While at first the hand drum seems to be playing the same rhythm throughout the example, there are slight deviations introduced that are in the form of a short syncopated pattern. Listen carefully to the drum part until you can hear these changes. Try to discover if there is any relationship between the changes and the voice part.

Q14   Do these deviations coincide with any particular events in the voices?
       a. No. The accompaniment is independent of the voices.
       b. Yes. The accompaniment changes noticeably when the voices first enter.

Example 7.12   G. Paxton and F. Guilbeau
                Your Gentle Ways of Loving Me (excerpt)
                20th-century American composers/performers

This piece gives us a chance to observe a solo and accompaniment in which a variety of rhythmic activity takes place at four different meter levels:

The tempo of the two-pulse basic meter is moderate, marked most consistently by the bass on the beginning of each pulse.

Q15   On which level does the voice operate? the harmonica? the drums?
   a. The voice operates on the slow level, the harmonica on the fastest, the drums on the basic pulse.
   b. The voice operates on the fast level, the harmonica on the fast, the drums on the basic pulse.
   c. The voice operates on the fast level, the harmonica on the slow, the drums on the fastest.

Q16   Besides marking the basic pulse, the bass sometimes uses another level. Which one?
   a. the slow level
   b. the faster level
   c. the fastest level

Q17   Following two verses, there is a brief contrasting conclusion. How does the rhythmic activity of the voice and bass change?
   a. Both move to the slow level.
   b. Both move the fastest level.
   c. The bass changes to the fastest level and the voice changes to the slow level.

> Find a songbook that gives accompaniment chords. Play the chords on piano, guitar, or autoharp, in rhythmic patterns as interesting as you can invent. If you don't play an instrument, make up the rhythm patterns and ask a friend to play them.

The Pitch Factor

In Chapter 6 we considered some of the ways in which tonal centers and conventions of pitch relationships are established. These often play an important part in the background role of an accompaniment, as in Examples 7.13–7.19.

Example 7.13   Traditional music from India
             Salutation Song (excerpt)

This piece employs a drone, one of the simplest and strongest ways to establish a tonal center as a background for other activity.

Q18   How many distinct pitches are audible in the drone?

    a. one

    b. two

    c. three

    d. four

Example 7.14   Frédéric Chopin
Piano Sonata No. 2, Funeral March (excerpt)
19th-century Polish composer

From a drone to a chordal accompaniment for a dominant melody can sometimes be a short step. In this excerpt each chord is stuck in the simplest of rhythmic patterns: one chord on each beat of the two-beat basic meter.

Q19   Does the two-chord pattern used in the accompaniment change in this example?

    a. Yes, it changes pitch and rhythm throughout.

    b. Yes, the pitch pattern changes near the end of the example. The rhythm remains constant throughout.

    c. No.

Example 7.15   Louis Moreau Gottschalk
The Dying Poet (excerpt)
19th-century American composer

Nearly as simple rhythmically is the "oom-pah-pah" accompaniment often heard in waltzes with the lowest pitch of the chord on the first pulse of the three-pulse basic meter and the remaining chord pitches on the other two pulses. This pattern is sustained throughout this excerpt.

In Examples 7.14–7.17 chordal support is generally continuous, but such support has a different role in *recitative,* a conversational or narrative element in many vocal works such as operas, oratorios, and cantatas. The chords accompanying a recitative are usually played by a keyboard instrument, and most often they punctuate the nonpulsed rhythm of the vocal line at irregular points in time.

Example 7.16   Frédéric Chopin
Ballade No. 1, Op. 23 (excerpt)
19th-century Polish composer

Like Example 7.15, this excerpt is a waltz, with a three-pulse basic meter. Following a nonpulsed introduction, you will be able to distinguish the three-pulse meter.

Examples 7.15 and 7.16 have many similarities. They are both piano pieces, in a three-pulse meter using an "oom-pah-pah" accompaniment.

Q20 Listen to Examples 7.15 and 7.16 again. How would you compare the use of the three-beat accompaniment?
    a. Both have the accented (first) beat in the lower voice.
    b. Both have the accented beat in the upper voice.
    c. 7.15 has the accented voice in the upper, 7.16 in the lower.
    d. 7.16 has the accented voice in the upper, 7.15 in the lower.

Example 7.17   *My Lord What a Morning* (excerpt)
                American music

In the three preceding examples the rhythm of the chordal accompaniment is extremely simple, with the chords tied to basic pulses only. Here, although the chords themselves are less complicated, their pitches are mostly strung out one after another in more active rhythmic patterns.

Q21 What new background element is added when the male voice enters?
    a. a high guitar part
    b. a dronelike bass part
    c. a bass line with continuous movement

Example 7.18   Johann Sebastian Bach
                Saint Matthew Passion, "Then Answered Peter"
                18th-century German composer

In this example three characters from the oratorio are having a lively musical discussion (in German). Listen to the chordal punctuation provided by the accompanying instruments. Notice the variance in lengths of time between the chord changes.

Example 7.19   Louis Armstrong
                Potato Head Blues (excerpt)
                20th-century American composer/performer

In jazz, a technique called stop-time is similar to the recitative concept. Listen to how the punctuations in the accompaniment complement what the soloist is "saying."

Q22 Compare the lengths of time between punctuations in Examples 7.18 and 7.19. What is the difference?
    a. They are both irregular (nonpulsed).
    b. They are both regular (pulse implied).

c. 7.18 is irregular, 7.19 is regular.

d. 7.18 is regular, 7.19 is irregular.

Rhythm and Pitch Together

The final examples of musical background are excerpts from two works in which rhythm and pitch together produce more active and complex accompaniments than we have heard so far.

Example 7.20   Antonin Dvořák
Symphony No. 9, third movement (excerpt)
19th-century Bohemian composer

After the opening unison passage, simple repeated chords in the strings support a fragmented principal melody in the woodwinds. Then the high strings take over the fragmented melody, supported by the winds and mid-range strings in a very active accompaniment. After a second unison passage, the strings play chord pitches one after another in the same rhythmic pattern. Then the full orchestra participates in various active accompaniment figures that support and compete for interest with the original melodic fragments.

Example 7.21   Gustav Mahler
The Song of the Earth, "Drinking Song of Earth's Sorrow" (excerpt)
19th/20th-century Austrian composer

The accompaniment in the preceding example is fairly complex, but not by comparison with this one, the richness of which is a giant leap from the simple accompaniments heard earlier. So much is going on in pitch structure, rhythmic patterns, and orchestral sounds that the entire accompaniment operates almost independently of the principal vocal line and places great demands on our attention.

Compose two or three melodies using the black keys of the piano. Add different kinds of accompaniment: a drone, a contrasting melody, chords on the black keys.

Do the same thing using all the keys of the piano.

SYNTHESIS

To summarize the ideas of this chapter, a portion of a movement of a symphony has been chosen in which clear examples of foreground-background relationships are evident. In Example 7.22, the sound sources are flutes, oboe, bassoon, upper-register strings, middle-register strings, and lower-register strings.

> **Example 7.22** Felix Mendelssohn
> *Symphony No. 4* ("Italian"), second movement (excerpt)
> 19th-century German composer

As you listen, focus on the following elements to hear when they occur:

1. a melody played in unison by the middle-register strings, oboe, and bassoon
2. the same melody played in a higher register by the upper-register strings
3. an independent bass line, played by the lower-register strings
4. a secondary melody played by the flutes

A diagram has been provided on page 156 to assist you in identifying the above elements. In the diagram, the following information is outlined to help identify the sections as they unfold. Melodic form (MF) shows where the principal melodies repeat (a–a), where they vary (a–a'), and where they change completely (a–b). Sound sources (SS) identify the instruments playing during the section. Texture (T) points out the principal and secondary melodies, and ostinato figures. Length (L) identifies the number of measures (groups of basic pulses) present in the section.

During Section 1, a short unison melody is interrupted by a bass ostinato.

> **Q23** How does the pace of the bass ostinato compare with that of the basic pulse?
> a. It is slower.
> b. It is faster.
> c. It is the same.

	Section 1	Section 2	Section 3	Section 4
MF	introduction	a	a′	a
SS	fls, ob, bsn, all strings	ob, bsn, ms, ls	same	us, fls, ls
T	unison melody	melody, bass ost.	same	mel, sec. mel, bass ost.
L	3 measures	4 measures	same	same

	Section 5	Section 6	Section 7	Section 8
MF	a′	b	a′	b
SS	same	ob, bsn, ms, ls	same	us, fls, ls
T	same	mel, bass ost.	same	mel, sec. mel, bass ost.
L	same	same	same	same

	Section 9	Section 10
MF	a′	c
SS	ob, bsn, fls, all strings	all strings
T	mel, sec. mel, bass ost.	mel, ostinato, bass ost. (with some pace variances)
L	3 measures, 2 pulses	9 measures, 2 pulses

KEY

MF—melodic form	bsn—bassoon
SS—sound sources	us—upper strings
T—texture	ms—middle strings
L—length	ls—lower strings
fls—flutes	same—no change from previous
ob—oboe	section (same element)

Section 3 is a melodic variation of Section 2.

Q24   Where does the melodic variation in Section 3 differ?
 a. all the way through
 b. in the first half
 c. in the middle
 d. in the second half

In Section 4 the upper strings enter repeating the melody played by the oboe, bassoon, and middle strings in Section 2.

Q25   How does the melody played by the upper strings differ?
    a. It doesn't differ, it is exactly the same.
    b. It is louder.
    c. It is in a higher register.
    d. It is in a lower register.

The bass ostinato begun in Section 1 remains virtually unchanged in pace for quite some time.

Q26   During what section is the pace of the bass ostinato briefly interrupted for the first time?
    a. Section 3
    b. Section 4
    c. Section 5
    d. Section 6

Compare the secondary melody played by the flutes in Sections 4 and 5. Pay particular attention to how the beginning and ending of the secondary melody compares with those of the principal melody.

Q27   How do the beginnings and endings compare?
    a. The principal and secondary melodies both begin together.
    b. The secondary melody begins before the principal melody.
    c. The secondary melody begins after the principal melody.

Q28   Compare the same elements in Sections 8 and 9. How do the beginnings and endings compare?
    a. The principal and secondary melodies both begin and end together.
    b. The instruments playing the secondary melody begin before the principal melody.
    c. The instruments playing the secondary melody begin after the principal melody.

At the beginning of Section 10 the pace of the bass ostinato is picked up by the middle strings.

Q29   What happens to the pace of the lower strings?
    a. It is slower.
    b. It is faster.
    c. It stays the same.
    d. It starts too unevenly to determine.

SUCCESSION
AND
GROWTH

Music can be perceived only as it unfolds in time. We can never have a whole musical work in our presence at a single moment as we can a painting. In this respect, a piece of music is more like a piece of sculpture; to sense the sculpture whole we must gather and fuse many perceptions, gained one after another, as the piece is viewed from various angles. This takes time. It is time we can spend as we choose, though—focusing here, concentrating there, secure in the knowledge that the sculpture will not move. But music moves inexorably, never allowing us to study the moment, never pausing for us to catch up. We need quick ears and, often, a good memory to deal with each moment as it goes by.

We can describe *growth* as the outcome of relationships between successive musical events. We might assume that all music is made up of such relationships, but many recent compositions seem to be simply successions of sound events, so that all we need to do is take in what

A piece of sculpture shot from the side, the back, and the front in the Museum of Modern Art's Sculpture Garden in New York. (*Family Group,* 1948–49, by Henry Moore Collection, The Museum of Modern Art New York)

happens as it happens, with little or no need to remember what has gone before or anticipate what may follow.

X Example 8.1   John Cage
            Variations II (excerpt)
            20th-century American composer

> This excerpt is from one version of a piece that could be performed in many very different ways, depending on how the performer (here, David Tudor) chooses to interpret the very open-ended directions of the "composer," John Cage. Tudor's version uses the electronic techniques of amplification and feedback to alter the sounds the piano can make. Cage says that such works represent "*dis*organization and a state of mind which in Zen is called no-mindedness." At most, any relationships between successive sound events seem to be incidental rather than central to the result.

Although the sound sources and composing-performing manner of Example 8.1 are contemporary, the idea of unrelated successions of musical events is not new. In many traditional vocal works music follows the flow of words in ever-changing ways (as in the recitative of Example 7.19). And in many improvisatory works—those composed as they are being performed (or designed to sound that way)—there is often much the same kind of flow of musical ideas with little interdependence.

X Example 8.2   Johann Sebastian Bach
            Organ Fantasia in G Minor (excerpt)
            18th-century German composer

> Although other parts of this piece are interdependent, this passage is one of several in which different ideas succeed each other in improvisatory style, without having much in common.

An important element in an improvisatory style is the presence or lack of presence of pulse. Sometimes the lack of a regular pulse adds to the sensation that the music is "free."

Q1   Is the Bach pulsed or nonpulsed?
     a. pulsed
     b. nonpulsed

Much of the music we hear, however, does involve relationships that we must notice if we are to follow the growth of a composition. This "art of noticing" requires the same kind of concentration needed to follow a debate or a lecture; a lapse in attention may mean losing an important train of thought, with the result that one's perception of the whole argument is incomplete or flawed.

Following the growth of a piece is like playing a game of expectations—expectations aroused, confirmed, delayed, denied. Here is a visual analogy:

Finding the number 2 in this design is like hearing the first musical event of a composition. With the 2 as a beginning, how will things proceed? Our expectation is that more numbers will follow, although we do not yet know if a design will emerge—that is, if the numbers will be random or ordered. What will the next number be?

Finding that the next number is 4 arouses some expectations and cancels others. Whatever the pattern is to be, it won't be one-after-one: 3 is missing. We still can't tell what the third number will be—6? 8? 7? Perhaps a return to 2? Perhaps a random number that would cancel our growing expectation of a continuing pattern? At this point, the possibilities are narrowing, and the tension of learning the outcome is high.

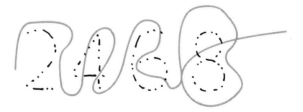

Now we know which possibility has been chosen, and the tension is released by a clear outcome. If, however, the fourth number had been 11 or 17, the firm expectation aroused by 6 would have been denied, the pattern broken, and tension raised to a new level by uncertainty.

No such analogy with music can be exact, but something like this does go on in the growth of compositions that depend on interrelationships. A composer is constantly generating expectations, then confirming, modifying, delaying, or denying them. In general, the more confirmation, the greater the sense of unity; variety tends to result from modification, delay, or denial. Following the balances between unity and variety in the growth of a piece can become one of the great joys of listening to music, for, as the philosopher R. G. Collingwood has said, to follow the work of a gifted artist is to share the gift. Before turning to a few examples that show how some composers have dealt with the growth of their musical ideas, we will list the four ways (broadly speaking) in which the small bits and pieces that make up those ideas can be treated.

1. by repetition (doing it again)

2. by variation (doing it differently)

3. by digression (doing something else)

4. by recurrence (returning to it)

MOTIVE, PHRASE, CADENCE, SECTION

A *motive* is the smallest germ of musical growth. It is a short, distinctive rhythmic-melodic figure that often forms a part of a longer unit. When first heard, the figure is not a motive, merely an idea. It *becomes* a motive as it is repeated, varied, or returned to as an integrating element.

The *phrase* is the next larger unit of growth. It is a musical idea more or less complete in itself, like a clause in a sentence. Phrases are concluded by *cadences,* endings that are similar to punctuation in writing. A cadence may convey a feeling of completion, functioning like a period at the end of a sentence,or a feeling of momentary pause with more to come, as with a comma. Often two phrases are linked together in a statement-response relationship, the statement ending with an intermediate cadence, the response with a cadence that gives a sense of completion. Often several phrases, in turn, grow into a musical *section,* sometimes complete in itself, sometimes open to continuation. If complete, the section may include digression and recurrence in a unity-variety process. Example 8.3 provides a good opportunity to follow the growth of a small musical unit through its use of a motive, its linkage of phrases, and its application of repetition, variation, digression, and recurrence to produce a highly unified yet gently varied whole.

Example 8.3   Antonin Dvořák
Symphony No. 9, second movement (excerpt)
19th-century Bohemian composer

The rhythmic diagram sets out the slow two-pulse basic meter. It also outlines the actual rhythm of the foreground melody in

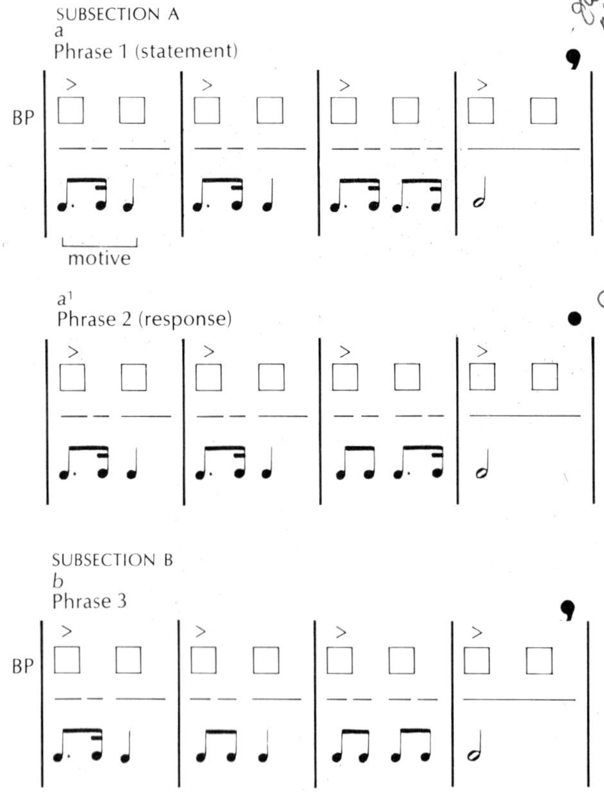

SUBSECTION A
a
Phrase 1 (statement)

BP

motive

a¹
Phrase 2 (response)

SUBSECTION B
b
Phrase 3

BP

STRUCTURE AND SHAPE

$\int$o far we have been concentrating primarily on individual musical events within a small span of a larger context—on the parts rather than the whole, somewhat as if we had isolated them in a vacuum. But now we turn at last to the composition as a whole, in which these individual events flow together into a total structure and shape.

The *structure* of a composition is its plan of organization, which provides an overall framework for the smaller succession and growth processes we looked at in Chapter 8. In this chapter we will be examining three different kinds of structure:

1. organic structure: a plan of organization that is unique to a particular piece
2. conventional structure: any one of many widely used patterns
3. open structure: a result created by the performer from options offered by the composer

During this chapter we will also be calling your attention to the *shape* of a composition, in which all the small tension-repose effects we have mentioned in earlier chapters come together into a beginning-to-end flow of tension, climax, and repose.

ORGANIC STRUCTURES

A work with an organic structure may be said to have its own growth-determining logic, with its composer allowing its musical events to develop in accordance with their own inherent nature. Such a piece is by no means a succession of unrelated musical events like those of Examples 8.1 and 8.2. Its growth is real and meaningful, with its moments very often related to one another. It might be better to call this kind of structure a *procedure* rather than an organizational plan. Examples 9.1 and 9.2 illustrate this kind of organic procedure.

Example 9.1   Luciano Berio
                Sinfonia, Section 4 (excerpt)
                20th-century Italian composer

Though it follows no traditional pattern, this piece is close-knit and logical; each moment evolves out of what has come before, creating a distinct and unique pattern.

Q1   Which factors contribute to the continuity of this piece?
      a. even pulse; unison passages
      b. use of organ and keyboard percussion throughout
      c. sustained sounds; whispers; vocal outbursts

Example 9.2   Johann Sebastian Bach
                Organ Toccata in D Minor
                18th-century German composer

This well-known example leaves a great deal of interpretive decisions up to the performer. Another recording of this same piece might sound quite different. Some of the factors of choice left to the performer include the timing of the phrases and silences, and the choice of registration (color of sound) in the organ.

Q2   Which factors contribute to the continuity of this piece?
      a. tempo and balance
      b. ostinato and variation
      c. motivic and tonal relationships

Does the structure of this painting seem arbitrary to you? Do the objects in it seem meaningfully related? The artist named it *Blue Package*—not *Eggs,* or *Paper Bag.* Why? (1970, by Claudio Bravo)

The device of *imitation* (as in Example 7.8) also tends to produce organic structures. In a very general way, imitation passes a musical idea from one line to another in contexts where there is a good deal of continuous, independent melodic activity in all lines. It may be strict and continuous, as in a round like "Frère Jacques," or as diverse as several ideas that go from line to line.

Example 9.3   G. F. Handel
"And With His Stripes," from *The Messiah* (excerpt)
18th-century German composer

Q3   How does Handel reflect the power of the word "healed"?
a. He states it only in a solo voice.
b. He quickens the pace each time the word is sung.
c. The word has the longest time value in the phrase.
d. He eliminates the instrumental accompaniment during the word.

CONVENTIONAL STRUCTURES

A convention is any method or practice that is in wide enough use to be generally understood and accepted. Among the many possible ways of organizing music, some patterns have proved so useful that they have enjoyed a long life in various guises within our culture, and have thus become conventions. Some belong to other cultures as well. The conventional structures we will discuss in this chapter are *recurrence, variation,* and *two-partness;* they are all based on distinctly recognizable *sections* of music, and they are all built on the same principles of repetition, variation, recurrence, and digression that we considered on a small scale in Chapter 8.

Recurrence: Refrain

Recurrence is a return to something after something else has taken place. Any musical structure based on recurrence must therefore have at least two different sections, one of which acts as a unifying force by recurring after one or more digressions. One of the simplest instances of recurrence is the verse-refrain pattern found so often in work songs and other folk songs. Though the music of all the verses remains the same in such songs, the different words for each verse supply a sense of digression; and the refrain, with the same music and words returning after each verse, supplies a sense of stability—a kind of repeated homecoming.

Example 9.4   Traditional American music   *verses & Refrain*
             Old Cold 'Tater (excerpt)

The excerpt includes Verse one, the Refrain (beginning with the words "Well an old cold 'tater'," Verse two, and the beginning of the Refrain.

Q4   Compare the first and the second refrains.
      a. They are exactly the same.
      b. They are slightly varied.
      c. They are extremely varied.

Example 9.5   Guillaume Costeley
             Go, Happy Shepherds (Allons, gai gai bergères)
             16th-century French composer

While Example 9.4 begins with the verse, this sixteenth-century French Christmas song begins with the refrain. This further emphasizes the role of the refrain as a stabilizing element that frames change from beginning to end, as the diagram shows:

Refrain	Verse 1	Refrain	Verse 2	Refrain
A	B	A	C	A
a b b		*b b^1*		*b b^1*

	Verse 3	Refrain	Verse 4	Refrain
	D	A	E	A^1
		b b^1		

Q5 In what way is the final refrain different from all the others?
   a. It is twice as long.
   b. It is sung at a faster pace.
   c. It changes to the major tonality; all the other refrains are in minor.

Example 9.6   *Here, Rattler, Here* (excerpt)
                  American music

This work begins with a two-phrase refrain, like a statement and response; each of the phrases is sung first by the soloist, then by the chorus. The rest of the song proceeds with one-line verses, each answered by the first and second phrases of the refrain, in turn:

Refrain	Verse 1 (solo)	Refrain (chorus)	Verse 2 (solo)	Refrain (chorus)
A (solo) A^1 (chorus)	B	A	B^1	A^1

	Verse 3 (solo)	Refrain (chorus)	Verse 4 (solo)	Refrain (chorus)
	B^2	A	B^3	A^1

The superscripts with the letters indicate some degree of change in the music; we will use this method throughout this chapter. As indicated, the music of each verse differs somewhat, because of the spontaneous changes improvised by the soloist. These changes heighten the stability of the recurring refrain, despite its own small changes, which the singers of the chorus also supply spontaneously.

Recurrence: Rondo

Many musical structures of varying size and complexity, in works from medieval love songs to contemporary rock, are based on the principle of recurrence in a way similar to the verse-refrain patterns of Examples 9.5 and 9.6: the same music is heard at beginning and end, and between each digression. One of these structures, called *rondo,* has at least two digressions, which differ not only from the recurring section but from each other as well, as in Example 9.7.

Example 9.7   Jean Philippe Rameau
Musette en rondeau
18th-century French composer

The recurring section of this piece uses a drone, in imitation of the small French bagpipe of the eighteenth century. The overall sectional structure may be outlined as follows:

$$\|: \quad \begin{matrix} A \\ a\ a^1 \end{matrix} \quad :\| \quad \begin{matrix} B \\ b\ b^1 \end{matrix} \quad \begin{matrix} A \\ a\ a^1 \end{matrix} \quad \begin{matrix} C \\ c\ c^1 \end{matrix} \quad \begin{matrix} A \\ a\ a^1 \end{matrix} \quad \begin{matrix} D \\ \end{matrix} \quad \|: \quad \begin{matrix} A \\ a\ a^1 \end{matrix} \quad :\|$$

The small letters refer to the two-phrase statement-answer pattern found in each section except D, which is longer and freer. Section D is also a culmination of the progressively greater contrast in Sections B and C. This increasing contrast is the cause of the increasingly greater sense of tension released with each unchanged return of A—one of the effects potentially inherent in any structure with a statement-digression-restatement arrangement.

Q6   What does the performer do to provide some variety in the repeated statements within Section A at the beginning and end?
   a. The performer changes the color of the harpsichord's sound.
   b. The performer varies the tempo with rubato.
   c. The performer pauses between the repeated statements.

Recurrence: Ternary Design

In all the preceding examples the recurring section has come back at least twice, following two or more digressions. We come now to a structure having a single return after one contrasting section. Customarily labeled *ternary design,* this structure has been used in a great variety of musical styles, and for pieces ranging in size from a short folk song to an entire symphonic movement.

Example 9.8   Hoagy Carmichael
Georgia on My Mind (excerpt)
20th-century American composer/performer

ABA¹? No, not really, but the picture certainly has some sort of ternary design. (*Bear in Tree,* 19 c., by an unknown American artist)

The structure of this tune can be summarized as:

Introduction   A   B   A¹
            a a¹   *b*   *a²*

Q7 In general, one expects the recurrence of a musical idea following a contrasting section to lower tension by returning to familiar ground, but in this case tension increases when A¹ begins. Why?
  a. A¹ is an instrumental section.
  b. Instead of returning to the initial melody, the singer varies it greatly, starting at a higher pitch level.
  c. Instead of returning to the initial melody, the singer varies it greatly, starting at a lower pitch level.
  d. The singer changes the words when A¹ begins.

Example 9.9   John McLaughlin
                Dawn
                20th-century American composer/performer

Despite their length and continuity, the three sections of this ternary structure (ABA¹), should be easy to distinguish. Following the introduction by electric piano, bass guitar, and drums, A has first a slow melody by violin and guitar, then a guitar solo that rises and falls in tension, reaching a peak at its end. This momentum carries into B, which is in a faster tempo; it opens with violin and guitar stating a complex rhythm three times, continues with a violin solo, and closes with the same complex rhythm with which it began. A^1 is a modified return of A; instead of coming to a stop, it simply fades away.

In terms of shape, prolonged tension occurs during the guitar solo and the violin solo; the energy of the complex rhythm adds to the tension, although the rhythm serves to stabilize B by both opening and closing it. A^1 is basically a section of repose, in which the tensions generated earlier are released. The whole tension-repose shape would look something like this:

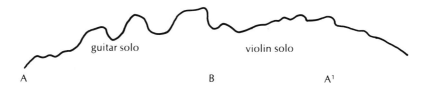

guitar solo   violin solo

A   B A^1

Compose a rhythm piece with a ternary structure, using any handy metal objects. Be sure your basic rhythmic patterns provide enough contrast to distinguish the two different sections clearly.

Improvise an ABACA rondo, using three different sound materials (for example, metal, wood, and glass) for the A, B, and C sections.

Recurrence: Sonata Form

A more complex structure based on the principle of recurrence is *sonata form*, most often found in one or more movements of such multimovement works as sonatas, symphonies, and string quartets. Though sonata form originated in a two-part structure (see page 197), it later took on the three-part structure of ternary design, with these divisions:

A	B	A^1
Exposition	Development	Recapitulation

Without going into detail about what may happen within any of these divisions—something the very nature of sonata form makes it all but impossible to do—we can abstract a scheme of a sonata-form movement:

Exposition			Development	Recapitulation
a	transition	*b* close	*a* and *b* or other ideas developed	*a* transition *b* close
(original pitch center)	(pitch center changing)	(new pitch center)	(changes of pitch center)	(usually original pitch center throughout)

This scheme hints at one of the central features of sonata form. contrast and conflict of pitch centers, with one pitch center (or tonic) solidly established at the beginning and end of the movement and a good deal of change in between, usually reaching a peak in the development section. To follow this pitch-center game often requires rather sophisticated listening ability. Here we note only that the game exists, and that learning to follow it is very rewarding.

The observations below about the three divisions of a sonata-form movement are necessarily as general as the scheme above, but they may be helpful by way of background before you listen to a complete sonata-form movement in Example 9.10.

1. *Exposition*. One or more strongly marked (and often contrasted) musical ideas are presented here, sometimes preceded by an introduction, sometimes not. A new pitch center is usually in force from the presentation of the second main idea through the end of the exposition. During the exposition one or more transitional passages appear, which are different in nature from the presentational quality of the main ideas, as is the closing passage. Even before the development section proper, these transitional and closing passages may develop the main ideas by fragmenting, expanding, or otherwise varying them. Often, the entire exposition section will be repeated.

2. *Development*. This section is the arena for the pitch-center game mentioned earlier. The development often opens with the same pitch center that was established at the end of the exposition and closes on the dominant of the original pitch center, in preparation for the recapitulation. The materials

of the development consist of at least one of the main ideas—or sometimes just one or more motives—that were presented in the exposition. No other generalizations about the development section are possible. There is no end to the number of ways in which musical ideas can be manipulated or new pitch centers introduced. By definition, the development section is full of surprises, and it is therefore, of course, the greatest source of tension in the movement.

3. *Recapitulation.* This section more or less straightforwardly repeats the materials of the exposition, although it usually hovers around the original pitch center throughout. This single pitch center is necessary here to lower the tension of the development section and to insure stability and repose for the end of the movement. The recapitulation may or may not be followed by a coda, a concluding passage with the paradoxical function of providing a suffix of continuing vitality at the end of the movement while it winds it down completely.

Example 9.10   Wolfgang Amadeus Mozart
Symphony No. 38 ("Prague"), third movement
18th-century Viennese composer

Listen to the movement several times, noting the divisions as they are announced on the recording. When you are familiar with it, try the following questions:

Q8   During the exposition, how does the transition function?
a. It glides smoothly from *a* to *b* without a break.
b. It interrupts for a new idea.
c. It interrupts for a further treatment of *a*.

Q9   Compare the musical character of *a* and *b*.
a. *b* is less aggressive.
b. *b* is more aggressive.
c. *b* is initially more gentle and then more aggressive.

Q10   How does the close of the exposition relate to the earlier material?
a. It is closely related to *b*.
b. It is entirely new.
c. It is closely related to *a*.

Q11   How does the material treated in the development relate to the
material in the exposition?
a. It is derived solely from *a*.
b. It is derived solely from *b*.
c. It is related to both *a* and *b*.
d. It is unrelated to either *a* or *b*.

Listen to the first movements of any two symphonies by
Haydn or Mozart. Devise some kind of graph or verbal
description that will help you recognize the similarities or
differences in the way sonata form is treated.

Variations

In Chapter 8 we mentioned the principle of variation as one of the four
basic ways in which composers treat their musical ideas during the
growth of a composition. This kind of variation of details can be found
in nearly all musical structures in all cultures. Now, though, we are
talking about variation as a musical structure in its own right, in
which a clearly defined musical unit—a small section, a complete tune,
a fixed set of chords, for example—is presented and then systemati-
cally varied a number of times to produce an entire movement or work,
with each variation forming a part of the whole. In Western culture
this procedure goes back at least as far as the Middle Ages, when
repetitions of a tune were often enhanced by improvised variations
of it.

Example 9.11   Anonymous
Chansonetta tedesca

This "little German song" of the fourteenth century is performed
on the shawm with an accompaniment of medieval fiddle and
drums. Following the drone-and-drum introduction the shawm
plays the tune in plain fashion. Then, after a brief fiddle-and-drum
interlude, it plays a variation of the tune.

From the sixteenth century to our own time, sets of variations on a
theme—often a popular tune—have been written in many styles but

with essentially the same structural plan. We will examine one such set in some detail.

Example 9.12   Franz Schubert
                Piano Quintet ("Trout"), fourth movement
                19th-century Viennese composer

Schubert took the theme of this movement from his song "The Trout," and wrote a set of six variations on it for piano, violin, viola, cello, and bass. The structure of the theme is a small ternary form:

$$\|: a\ a^1 :\|\ :\|: b :\|\ a^2 :\|$$

This form is retained in each variation, all of which are self-contained, except for the link between Variations 5 and 6. Every variation puts the theme in a new context.

Variation 1: The piano ornaments the theme, the bass plays a pizzicato (plucked) line, and the other three strings play short, darting figures, sometimes imitating the piano trills.

Q12   What is the primary role of the piano?
       a. It plays a rhythmic accompaniment.
       b. It plays block chords.
       c. It plays a bass line.
       d. It plays an ornamental melody.

Variation 2: The cello plays the melody, imitated by the piano. The high violin part is a very active, decorative melody moving at a faster pace than the other instruments.

Q13   What is the role of the bass in this section?
       a. It plays an independent melody.
       b. It plays part of the background chords.
       c. It plays a variation of the theme.
       d. It is not playing in this section.

Variation 3: The bass plays the theme, joined by the cello at a couple of phrase ends, while the piano takes over the brilliant decorative melodic role the violin had in Variation 2. Its strength almost overshadows the theme.

Q14   During Variation 3, what is the role of the violin and viola?
       a. They play a rhythmic accompaniment.
       b. They play the melody.
       c. They play sustained chords.
       d. They do not play in this section.

Variation 4: There is an abrupt shift in mood and in treatment of the theme. Both the bold chords at the beginning and the lighter, active interplay later almost completely obscure the theme itself.

Q15 During Variation 4, what is the role of the bass?
  a. It is active on nearly every pulse.
  b. It sustains long notes.
  c. It is melodic.

Variation 5: The cello solo is once again clearly related to the theme, though considerably changed as compared with Variations 2 and 3. In the second part of the variation the pitch center moves far from the original tonic; for this reason the extension is needed to get back to the tonic for the final variation.

Variation 6. The theme returns in a plain, undecorated version, with an accompaniment that brings back the darting figures of Variation 1. The original structure is stretched out by repeating the *b* and a^2 portions, which are followed by a brief concluding extension.

Q16 Which two instruments share the theme?
  a. violin and viola
  b. violin and piano
  c. violin and cello
  d. violin and bass

Q17 Which two instruments exchange the darting figure?
  a. violin and viola
  b. violin and piano
  c. violin and cello
  d. violin and bass

The shape of the whole set of variations is reasonably clear: a low-level beginning with the simple theme, a heightened level of similar activity in Variations 1 and 2; that level raised higher with the brilliance of Variation 3, a peak of tension in the opening of Variation 4, and then a slow relaxation toward the repose of the theme's simplicity in Variation 6:

V.1   V.2   V.3   V.4   V.5   V.6

A wedding quilt, made in 1876 and found in Vermont. If the scene in the center is the theme, what are the twelve outer sections?

Compose a theme and variations using spoken sounds only. Construct the theme from a pattern of words. Develop variations by modifying the sounds of the words, changing the word order, using contrasting vocal sounds, or adding a percussion accompaniment.

Two-Partness

The third structural pattern that has been used widely enough to be regarded as a convention is the division of a piece into two distinct parts. The relationship between the two parts can be one of sharp contrast or one of close-knit continuity of shared materials, with any number of shadings between these extremes. Examples 9.13–9.16 provide a small sampling of the possibilities.

Example 9.13   Henry Purcell
Dido and Aeneas, Overture
17th/18th-century English composer

The distinction in mood and character between the two parts of this work is clearly marked—the first part slow and serious, the second much livelier. Each section grows in seamless fashion out of its own single basic idea. The first section is not repeated, the second is; here is the overall structure:

A :‖ B :‖

The eighteenth-century Connecticut gravestone of four young brothers. Do you see a parallel between its structural pattern and one of the musical structures discussed in this chapter?

Many pieces of the seventeenth and eighteenth centuries—including innumerable dance pieces—are in two parts with each part repeated. In some, the musical materials of the two parts differ:

‖: A :‖: B :‖

In many others the two sections share the same materials:

‖: A :‖: A¹ :‖

In both cases the two-partness is emphasized by strong cadences at the end of each section and by the repetition of each section.

> **Example 9.14**   William Byrd
> *Earl of Salisbury's Pavan*
> 16th/17th-century English composer

In this dance (intended more for listening than for dancing) each section has different musical material. The performer provides some variety in the repetitions by changing the sound of the harpsichord.

> **Example 9.15**   George Frideric Handel
> *Flute Sonata,* Op. 1, No. 11, second movement
> 18th-century German composer

The two sections of this movement share the same musical ideas. Each section begins with the same figure, followed by a few short phrases, and concludes with a much longer and more active phrase. The shape can be shown like this:

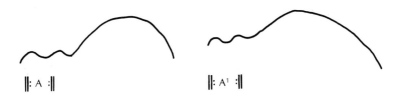

‖: A :‖   ‖: A¹ :‖

Mixed Structures

Within a single piece, composers often use more than one of the conventional structures we have been examining. The different kinds of two-partness we saw in Examples 9.14 and 9.15, for instance, came to be modified by the principle of recurrence, producing a combination of two- and three-partness called *rounded binary,* the source of sonata form. Two of the possible rounded binary schemes are

$$\begin{array}{ccc} A & A^1 \\ \|\text{:}\ a\ \text{:}\|\text{:}\ a^1\ a\ \text{:}\| \end{array} \qquad \text{or} \qquad \begin{array}{ccc} A & B \\ \|\text{:}\ a\ \text{:}\|\text{:}\ b\ a^1\ \text{:}\| \end{array}$$

Example 9.16   Wolfgang Amadeus Mozart
            Symphony No. 35 ("Haffner"), third movement
            18th-century Viennese composer

In the diagram of this movement below, the capital letters show the overall ternary design, and the small letters show the two-part substructures within it. (The diagram is incomplete: you will complete it yourself when you answer Q19.)

$$\begin{array}{ccccc} A & A^1 & B & & AA^1 \\ \|\text{:}\ a\ \text{:}\|\text{:}\ a^1\ a\ \text{:}\|\text{:}\ b\ \text{:}\|\text{:}\ ?\ \ ?\ \text{:}\|\ a\ a^1\ a\ \text{:}\| \end{array}$$

Each of the main sections A and B is a separate minuet, one of the most common eighteenth-century dances. At the time this movement was composed, it was customary to repeat the final *a* and a^1–*a* sections. Present-day performances eliminate this repetition, however, so that the two-partness of this final section disappears.

Q18   Which scheme represents the missing small letters in the B
       section?
       a. a^1–*a*
       b. b^1–b
       c. *a–b*
       d. *c–b*

Example 9.16 has a rather simple mixture of two structural patterns, but the mixture in Example 9.14 is considerably more intricate.

Example 9.17   Franz Joseph Haydn
            Piano Sonata, H. 43, third movement
            18th-century Viennese composer

The main sections form a clear rondo—ABACADA—and you may want to listen first for this plan of digression-recurrence. To aid you, each section is announced as it begins.

You may have discovered in listening that no two of the recurrences of A are quite alike. Each is varied, but not simply and straightforwardly as in the Schubert quintet movement (Example 9.12). The following outline is complex, but if you will stay with it while listening to the movement several times, you will hear some of the subtleties a skilled composer can bring to bear in fusing three structural conventions: rondo, variations, and ternary design.

A	B A^1	C A^2	D A^3	Coda
$a\ a^1\ b\ a\ a^1$	$a\ a^1\ \begin{cases} a\ a^1\ b\ a\ a^1 \\ \text{variation 1} \end{cases}$	$\begin{cases} a\ a^1\ b\ a\ a^1 \\ \text{variation 2} \end{cases}$	$a\ a^1\ \begin{cases} a\ a^1\ b\ a\ a^1 \\ \text{variation 3} \end{cases}$	

A few more comments may help:

1. In A, a and a^1 are two short phrases in a statement-response relationship.
2. In A^1 Haydn begins with an exact recurrence of a-a^1, leading us to expect an unchanged return to A before denying that expectation by launching into a variant.
3. In A^2 variation is begun at once, with no expectation of exact return.
4. A^3 begins with the identical pitches of A and A^1 but shifts to a lower register, referring subtly to the beginning of B, which started in the same way.

The shape of the piece is closely related to the sectional structure. Within A there is a small rise and fall of tension in the statement and response of a-a^1, while the length and contrast of b raise more tension, released by the return to a-a^1. Section B has considerable change; consequently, its level of tension increases.

Section C reaches the highest point of tension with more contrast than anything that has come before.

Section D starts out as a conclusion, but the surprise of its continuation provides new impetus and a fresh source of tension, released finally by the concluding recurrence of A^3 and the brief coda.

Q19   In which variation of A do you hear singular interjections of high-register pitches?

    a. A^1

    b. A^2

    c. A^3

Q20   Which of the following statements best reflects the relationship between musical structures and tension/repose?
   a. Repeated recurrences of a theme heighten tension.
   b. Repeated recurrences of a theme heighten repose.
   c. The recurrence of a theme after new material is introduced provides tension.
   d. The recurrence of a theme after new material is introduced provides repose.

OPEN STRUCTURES

All the preceding examples in this chapter have come to the moment of performance in some pre-established form, and whatever changes occur from one performance to another are matters of detail—different interpretations of how the composer intended the written notes of a composition to sound, or improvised contributions that are part of a given style, such as jazz. But the fundamental structure of them all remains the same, time after time. Not so with many pieces of our own time, in which composers ask performers to make choices that guarantee the piece will never be performed in exactly the same way twice. This process allows for possibilities that would probably not have occurred to the composer; but even if they had—a highly unlikely situation—the composer could not have notated them exactly. Such pieces are something like mobiles; their materials are meant to be open to constantly shifting relationships. Some offer the performer(s) only a narrow set of choices, while others present an almost unlimited invitation to improvise. Example 9.18 illustrates not *the* structure and shape of Earle Brown's piece, but one possible version that resulted from one particular set of choices made on one particular occasion. The performance you will hear is a once-only event.

Example 9.18   Earle Brown
               Piece for Any Number of Anythings (excerpt)
               20th-century American composer

Brown's "score" (opposite) describes five kinds of activity, each of which is improvised by the performers. A conductor (in this recording, Brown) makes the necessary choices: which activity will come when, how long it will last, how loud it will be, etc.

Get a group of fellow students or friends together and perform this piece. Use instruments or voices; take turns at conducting, making sure that whatever signals you need to use for start-stop, loud-soft, and fast-slow are simple and clear. Be imaginative and try for interesting outcomes.

Score By Earle Brown For His *Piece For Any Number Of Anythings*

1	2	3	4	5
long high notes	quick angular melodic lines	very legato lines	highly fragmented lines	very small noisy sounds on instruments*
slowly changing melodic lines	abrupt dynamic changes (normal sounds but vary timbre*— pizzicato, arco, etc.)	note-to-note intervals no more than a perfect fifth	note-to-note intervals always more than one octave!	
small intervals				
	vary durations			

*Timbral conditions may be translated into comparable or similar sounds from voices.

10

TENSION
AND REPOSE:
A SUMMARY

In Chapters 1–8 we often asked
you to notice specific details in terms of their capacity to generate
tension and repose, and in Chapter 9 we noted how cycles of tension
and repose determine the shape of a composition. Because tension and
repose cycles result from an intricate cause-and-effect network, they
are elusive. Because they are at the center of our response to music, it
is well worth devoting this final chapter to them.

CONDITIONING AND ATTITUDE

Tension and repose cycles work on two levels. The simpler level is the
effect of a sound wave on the human eardrum and nervous system. On
this level the response of any group of listeners who share the same
cultural conditioning will probably be similar: an extreme of any kind

will increase tension, and moderation of that extreme will decrease it. Loud and soft are one pair of extremes—the intensity of high amplification or the hush of a barely audible sound. Other pairs are slow and fast; high and low; complex and simple—more information than the ear can take in or less than it can tolerate. A more subtle pair of extremes is great or little change within any of the other pairs. There are no absolutes—tension and repose are always relative—and there are individual differences, of course, in degree of response. But in talking about extremes and their moderation, we can be reasonably sure that there will be more similarity than difference in their tension–repose impact on any group of listeners with a culture in common.

Find a few pieces that involve some of the extremes mentioned. Share them with friends who are not study-ing music and test our assumption of common cultural response.

One kind of tension-getting extreme—too much information. (Boston, Massachusetts)

The second level—the one that most concerns us—is much more subtle, complex, and personal. We can express it as an equation:

$$\text{music} \times (\text{perception} + \text{attitude}) = \text{tension-repose response}$$

The unknown variable in this equation is *you*. The more involved your attitude and the sharper your perception, the larger your musical "product" will be.

SOURCES OF TENSION AND REPOSE

By way of preface to the musical examples in this chapter, try the following experiments:

1. Strike or pluck a single sound on a piano (hold the key down), guitar, violin, vibraharp, gong, or similar instrument. Listen to the sound until it disappears completely. Which part of this experience is tension? Which part is repose?
2. Use the same sound source, but this time ask a friend to produce the sound. As it starts, clench your fist and take a deep breath. As it decays, slowly open your hand and exhale. This should help suggest how it is possible to become intimately wrapped up in a tension–repose cycle of sound.
3. Finally, still using the same sound source, turn your back to it. Ask your friend to play the sound for you several times at irregular intervals over a span of three to five minutes, responding as you did in the preceding experiment. What new variable affects your perception of tension and repose?

Though these exercises are elementary, they should demonstrate that even the simplest acoustical phenomenon—the single sound—is a source of tension and repose.

> By yourself or with one or more members of your class, perform John Cage's 4′33″. Be sure to perform the entire work! After the performance consider this question: where is the tension and where is the repose?

Expectation and Surprise

From all the preceding experiences you will probably have discovered that two of the most potent sources of tension are ambiguity and the unexpected. Conversely, clarity and the appearance of the expected are sources of repose. The question is, what *is* the expected? What makes a moment ambiguous? The answer lies in our conditioning—once we have enough experience with the kind of music at hand, we will know its probabilities or possibilities, and we will recognize a surprise when it comes. Examples 10.1–10.5 will help to illustrate expectation and surprise.

Example 10.1   *Alegrias* (excerpt)
               Flamenco music

The extraordinary length, intensity, and high range of the opening vocal passage fly in the face of "normal" expectation and create a high level of tension—probably due in part to the listener's almost physical identification with the singer's effort. The short phrases following seem more customary in length and effort, and thus provide a measure of repose.

Q1   Does the concluding vocal passage further relax the tension or
      raise it to a new level?
      a. It relaxes tension.
      b. It does not change the tension level.
      c. It raises tension to a new level.

Example 10.2   Johann Sebastian Bach
               Brandenburg Concerto No. 4, first movement (excerpt)
               18th-century German composer

In this work, as in Example 10.1, tension is generated through unexpected length. The piece opens with two balancing phrases of equal length, each lasting for six three-pulse basic-meter groups. This phrase pair is followed by an unpredictably long unbroken phrase, which lasts for *ten* three-pulse groups. This phrase raises the tension considerably. Then the first two balancing phrases return with the kind of stabilizing, repose-generating effect characteristic of any recurrence after contrast.

Q2   Is the phrase that follows this recurrence again long and
      unbalanced or is it the same length as the opening phrase?
      a. It is long and unbalanced.
      b. It is the same length as the opening phrase.

Q3 Is this phrase longer or shorter than the ten-group phrase?
   a. It is longer—twice as long, in fact.
   b. It is the same length.
   c. It is shorter.

Q4 What effect does the length of this phrase have on tension?
   a. It increases tension.
   b. It has a calming effect because of its length.
   c. It has no effect on the level of tension.

Example 10.3   Wolfgang Amadeus Mozart
              Variations on "Ah, vous dirai-je, Maman" (theme)
              18th-century Viennese composer

This is the same tune as "Twinkle, Twinkle Little Star." The
pitches for those four words form the first part of a two-part phrase.
They create tension by raising certain expectations: that the
second part will be equal in length to the first; that the rising
pitches of the first part will be answered by descending pitches in
the second; and that the second part will return to the tonic pitch,
with which the first began. All these expectations are fulfilled, and
a small tension–repose cycle is completed.

Q5 The two-part phrase described above is immediately repeated. Does
   this raise or lower tension? Why?
   a. It raises tension, because the repetition pushes the listener past
      the point of tolerance.
   b. It raises tension because the listener expects variation.
   c. It lowers tension because of the repose of repetition.

Q6 After this repetition, a contrasting two-part phrase is introduced.
   The second part of this new phrase is a slightly varied repetition of
   the first part. What tension-repose effects are provided by the
   slight variation?
   a. The variation raises tension.
   b. The variation lowers tension.
   c. The variation has no effect on the tension level.

Example 10.4   Ernst von Dohnányi
              Variations on a Nursery Song (theme)
              19th/20th-century Hungarian composer

This is another version of the tune in Example 10.3. The difference
between the two reveals a little more about expectation and
surprise and their tension-repose impact. It also illustrates a point
we mentioned earlier: the more musical information the listener

must take in, the greater the tension generated. With this in mind, compare the first statement of the first two-part phrase in each version. It is obvious that the Mozart has more information— a foreground melody and a background accompaniment. The Dohnányi has only the melody, doubled at the octave.

Q7   Which version has more new information, and therefore more tension, in the repetition of the first phrase?
     a. the Mozart
     b. the Dohnányi

Now compare the contrasting two-part phrase in each version, and the return to the opening phrase of each.

Q8   What elements in the Dohnányi provide the tension-creating surprises?
     a. the gradual quickening of the pace and the use of the trombone
     b. the use of rubato, changing harmony, and bassoon
     c. the sudden dynamic changes and the use of the harpsichord

Example 10.5   Wolfgang Amadeus Mozart
                   String Quintet, K. 515, second movement (excerpt)
                   18th-century Viennese composer

In this piece Mozart plays a quite sophisticated game of expectations. The structural outline below shows the basic binary plan. Unlike most such designs, however, every phrase is derived from the very first one; hence all the *a's,* with each numeral indicating a new variant.

$$\text{A} \qquad \text{B} \qquad \text{A}^1$$
$$\lVert\colon\; a\; a^1\; \colon\rVert\quad a^2\; a^3\; a^4\quad a^5\; a^6\; a^7\; a^8$$

Throughout, the continuing presence of the opening phrase is a stabilizing factor, tending toward repose. Except for the tension-lowering effect of the immediate repetition of a-a^1, however, this stability is more than counterbalanced by unpredictable changes that make each phrase different in some significant way from all the others.

Q9   Like most listeners, you very likely expect phrase a to be answered by a phrase of equal length. How does Mozart raise the tension by denying your expectation?

    a. He makes the answering phrase (a^1) half again as long.

    b. He makes the answering phrase (a^1) twice as long.

    c. He makes the answering phrase (a^1) twice as short.

Q10   Phrases a^2 and a^3 are related to a and a^1. What elements of a^3 raise the tension further?

    a. a^3 is slower and softer.

    b. a^3 begins in a different tonality than a^2.

    c. a^3 is longer still than a^1 and more complex in density.

Q11   Phrases a^5 and a^6 are a recurrence of a and a^1, with the same length relationship. What changes prevent them from providing the repose of an exact recurrence?

    a. The register is changed.

    b. The register is changed and played by a single instrument.

    c. The register is changed and the tonality shifts.

    d. The register is changed and more material is added to accompany the melody.

Q12   What expectation aroused by a and denied by a^1 is finally fulfilled by a^7 and a^8?

    a. a^8 returns to the tonic pitch.

    b. a^7 and a^8 are equal in length.

    c. a^8 is an exact repetition of a.

Q13   Which phrase reaches the highest level of tension because of the complexity of its contents—the number of things to take in simultaneously?

    a. a^1

    b. a^4

    c. a^6

    d. a^8

Repetition

Examples 10.1–10.5 have used repetition or recurrence in ways that provided stability and, thus, relative repose. But repetition can produce the opposite effect, too. If it is insistent—if it is carried past a listener's own point of tolerance—it can be a source of unbearable tension. In an Indian raga, for example, the constant repetition of the tonic by the drone of the tamboura—sometimes for an hour or more—can have one of two effects: it can cause an unattuned listener a certain amount of discomfort, or it can provide an ultimate sense of repose if the listener has come to terms with the nature of the music.

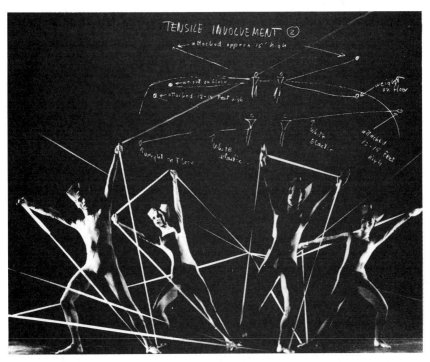

A still from the Nikolais Dance Theatre's production of "Tensile Involvement." The choreographer's notes indicate the position of the weights necessary to produce maximum tension in both the broad bands of elastic and the danders' bodies.

Example 10.6   Terry Riley
In C (excerpt)
20th-century American composer/performer

Though vastly different from the drone of an Indian raga, insistent repetition is the core of this work. The excerpt is a brief portion of a piece that can go on in this manner for forty-five to ninety minutes, as determined by the performers. How do you respond to it? Does the tension of repetition drive you out of the experience within a few seconds? Is the excerpt long enough for you to be liberated from the tension and relax into the curious effect of a kind of zero gravity?

Examples 10.7 and 10.8 use repetition in more involved or more ambiguous ways than *in C,* now generating, now releasing tension.

Example 10.7   Mick Jagger and Keith Richards
            Silver Train (excerpt)
            20th-century English composer/performer

An ostinato figure on the tonic chord begins this piece and is repeated many times, building up considerable tension. In fact, no change occurs for almost a full minute. When the dominant chord arrives we are momentarily released from the tension of the insistent tonic, but then another build-up of tension begins that does not subside until the original ostinato *returns* toward the end of the excerpt. Do you hear the piece this way?

Example 10.8   Igor Stravinsky
            The Rite of Spring, "Dance of the Adolescents" (excerpt)
            20th-century Russian composer

Like most introductions, the brief introductory passage in this excerpt raises some tension in anticipation of what is to follow. A stabilizing element is then established—a clocklike pulse, on which there is shortly superimposed a driving rhythm with unpredictably erratic pulse groups. This passage, dramatic and tension-filled, drops out, returns, drops out again, returns again. Though never quite the same, its recurrences become a stable factor, gradually changing the impact of the passage from high tension to moderate repose.

The tension-repose cycles of Examples 10.1–10.8, though very different in size and in degree of impact, all result from surprises sprung, and expectations aroused that are denied or fulfilled. But Example 10.9 is another matter altogether.

Example 10.9   Robert Ashley   *minimalist*
            She Was a Visitor (excerpt)
            20th-century American composer

No amount of experience with more conventional music is likely to help you in a piece like this. When you first hear it, you may not be able to sense any predictability or any source of repose—only the perpetual tension of a continuous stream of musical moments in constant change behind the insistently repeated foreground words. But continuity and a measure of repose are here, and you will find it rewarding to listen to the piece until you can sense its own unique flow of tension raised and lowered.

Choose a recording at random and try to discover its sources of tension and repose. List all the ways you can think of in which tension is generated.

Listen to your favorite piece of music and do the same thing.

Listen to your instructor's favorite piece of music and do the same thing.

Other Sources

Examples 10.10–10.13 illustrate several other sources of tension-repose cycles—provided one notices them.

Example 10.10   Béla Bartók
Concerto for Orchestra, fifth movement (excerpt)
20th-century Hungarian composer

This excerpt is in six sections:

1. a fanfare-like passage for brass
2. a long, active passage primarily for strings
3. a simpler passage for full orchestra, with some broad gestures
4. the same kind of activity as in Section 2, with fuller instrumentation
5. the gestures of Section 3, extended
6. a simple tune played by woodwinds, supported by strings and triangle

Q14   Why does the sustained sound in Section 1 create tension?
   a. It is a variation of the opening.
   b. It gets softer just as you expect it to get louder.
   c. It comes as a surprise, its instrumentation is different, and its pitch doesn't "fit" the pitch relationships of the passage as a whole.

Q15   What factors contribute to rising tension in Section 2?
   a. gradual increase in loudness; length and increased activity

    b. sameness of instrumentation and volume

    c. the overload of musical information

Q16   Does Section 3 provide more or less tension than Section 2? Why?

    a. More, because it is faster.

    b. More, because the density is greater.

    c. Less, because of the tranquillity of the melody.

    d. Less, because its simplicity relieves the nervous energy built up in Section 2.

Q17   Does Section 4 create repose, tension, or both, in relation to what has gone before?

    a. Repose, because it is a return of the kind of activity of Section 2.

    b. Tension, because of the variation of the added instruments.

    c. Repose, through return to the kind of activity of Section 2; tension through added instruments.

Q18   Sections 3 and 5 begin similarly. Which reaches a higher level of tension?

    a. Section 3, because it is the first time we have heard this material.

    b. Section 5, through an unexpected extension in relation to Section 3.

    c. Section 5, because it is much shorter and more dense than Section 3.

Q19   Does Section 6 bring more repose or greater tension?

    a. More repose, because of its comparative simplicity.

    b. More repose, because the brass instruments do not play.

    c. Greater tension, because of the fast-moving melody.

    d. Greater tension, because we are expecting a return of an earlier passage.

Example 10.11   Iannis Xenakis
                 Akrata (excerpt)
                 20th-century Greek composer

This excerpt uses three kinds of brass sounds: rapidly tongued pitches, sustained straight tones, and (later) the rough growl of flutter-tonguing.

Q20   Which set of musical elements could be described as tension-decreasers in this example?

    a. the surprise of silence and uncertainty about its length; sudden loud, sustained tone; onset of flutter-tonguing

b. unexpected silences; repetition of similar sounds; homogeneity of brass tones

c. repetition of similar sounds; soft, sustained passage; quiet conclusion

Example 10.12   Mort Dixon and Ray Henderson
Bye Bye Blackbird (excerpt)
20th-century American composer/performer

Example 10.13   Dixon and Henderson
Bye Bye Blackbird (excerpt)

Example 10.12 is from the record *Round about Midnight* by the Miles Davis Quintet; Example 10.13 is from *Miles Davis in Person*. A comparison of these two versions of the same song, played by the same principal artist, shows what differences in tension level can be created by two interpretations. The tune may be outlined as follows:

Introduction   phrase a phrase a^1 phrase b phrase a^2

Q21   Which version strikes you as the simpler, more straightforward presentation of the tune?
a. Example 10.12
b. Example 10.13

Q22   What overall factors in 10.13 create a level of tension somewhat higher than the level in 10.12?
a. a higher-pitched tonal center; larger group
b. a much longer introduction; unstable pulse groupings
c. more rhythmic energy, more variation

Q23   In which version does the introduction have a greater measure of tension? Why?
a. Example 10.12. There is no sense of how long it will last and where the melody will begin.
b. Example 10.13. The piano part is more complex, and the drums add momentum.

Q24   Compare phrase a in the two versions. What surprise raises the tension in 10.13?
a. The melody suddenly drops out.
b. The piano takes over the melodic line.
c. The rhythm stops.
d. The trumpet improvises on the melody.

Does the tension level of this painting seem very high to you or very low? Are any of the ideas in this chapter helpful in making or explaining your choice? (*The Whitestone Bridge,* 1939, by Ralston Crawford)

Q25   Why do phrases *b* and a^2 of 10.13 have a higher tension level than the same phrases in 10.12?
   a. The listener is expecting an exact recurrence.
   b. The meter shifts in the accompaniment.
   c. The trumpet sound is uniquely different.
   d. There is more variation, together with a higher pitch level, and more unexpected pitches.

Placido Domingo and Hildegard Behrens in the opera *Tosca* in tension. . .

. . . and in repose.

Invent any device, gadget, or project—no matter how farfetched—that convinces you personally of the validity of the ideas in this chapter

The end of this book merely marks a beginning. Music is a vast and continually expanding art that resists any effort to "explain" it or freeze it in words. Its logic is *musical,* not verbal. In your day-to-day listening you will encounter much music that relates to the topics in this book. You will also encounter much that does not. But in the latter case, you will not be at a loss if you have succeeded in opening your ears and sharpening your intuition. After all, listening to music is ultimately a matter of intuition. It is also one of life's most personal and enriching experiences.

GLOSSARY

This glossary is only a sampling of the terms you will encounter in reading about music. Consult any good dictionary of music for the definition of terms not found here.

Accelerando   increasing the tempo or speed

Aerophones   a class of instruments that generate sound by vibrating a stream of air

Aesthetics   a branch of philosophy dealing with theories of beauty and artistic values

Airchest   the chamber of an organ where air is stored to be released to individual pipes

Amplitude   the psychoacoustic term for loudness; measured in decibels

Angklung   a rattle-type idiophone made from bamboo or metal

Aria   a lyrical vocal solo common in opera, oratorios, and cantatas

Aulos   an ancient, two-piped aerophone

Ballade   a single-movement instrumental work, usually for piano

Ballad   a song or poem in storylike form

Bansuri   a bamboo flute used in Indian music

Blockflöte   the German name for the recorder

Brass   a Euro-American class of instruments that includes trumpet, French horn, trombone, and tuba

Bridge a rigid device used to lift the strings of a chordophone off the body of the instrument

Cadence the chords at the end of a composition or of a phrase or section within it

Cantata a vocal solo or choral work, secular or religious, of several movements

Capriccio Italian term suggesting animated or lively music

Choir a large choral ensemble whose repertoire is usually sacred

Chord the combination of two or more pitches

Chordophones a class of instruments that generate sound by vibrating a fixed cord, or string

Chorus a large choral ensemble; also, a choral composition

Chromelodeon an organlike instrument built by Harry Partch

Circular breathing a special playing technique used by some wind players whereby air stored in the cheeks is blown into the instrument while new air is drawn into the lungs through the nose

Concerto a large instrumental work in several movements that features one or more soloists and an orchestra

Decibel the unit of measurement for amplitude (loudness)

Diction the study and practice of pronunciation

Dominant chord a chord built on the fifth step of the scale

Drone a sustained, more or less fixed, accompaniment

Dulcimer a zither-type chordophone with a fretted fingerboard

Electrophones a class of instruments that generate sounds electronically

Fantasia an improvisatory instrumental work with no specific form

Flauto dolce the Italian name for the recorder

Frequency the rate of vibration of a sound, in hertz or cycles per second—the scientific equivalent of pitch

Fundamental tone the lowest pitch in a sound that includes harmonics

Gamelan an ensemble from Southeast Asia consisting of gongs, drums, xylophones, and strings

Glissando a continuous slide from one pitch to another

Habanera a Latin dance rhythm

Harmonics pitches occurring at frequencies that are whole-number multiples to a fundamental pitch

Harpsichord a type of keyboard chordophone in which the strings are plucked by a mechanical plectrum controlled by a key

Hemiola a regrouping of beats from 3 + 3 to 2 + 2 + 2; common in Hispanic music

Hertz the scientific unit of measurement for frequency; one hertz is equivalent to one cycle per second (cps)

Homophony a single-line musical dominance with accompanying parts

Hsiao a type of aerophone used in China

Idiophones a class of instruments that generate sound by vibrating the actual material of the instrument

Imitation a musical technique that features a single musical idea passed from one part to another

Keyboard instruments a class of instruments that use a keyboard, such as the piano, organ, harpsichord, clavichord, and synthesizer

Larynx the part of the human voice that contains the vocal cords

Mass a choral form based on the text of the Ordinary section of the Roman Catholic Mass

Mazurka a Polish dance rhythm

Melody the equivalent of a tune or complete musical idea

Membranophone a class of instruments that generate sound when a membrane is vibrated by being struck or placed into motion

Meter the organization of pulses into groups of twos and threes through the use of accents

Monophony a single-line musical texture

Musette a piece built on a drone designed to imitate the sound of a bagpipe

Mute a device applied to an instrument to soften its sound or alter its tone

Nocturne a mood piece that evokes the feeling of night

Octave a pitch that vibrates at a $2:1$ (or multiple of $2:1$) ratio with a reference pitch

Opera a theatrical/musical composition with vocal solos and ensembles, dramatic action, and orchestra

Oscillator an electronic device that produces pitches; also known as a tone generator

Ostinato a rhythmic pattern that repeats constantly

Overture an orchestral piece that precedes a long theatrical work such as an opera; also an independent orchestral work of a programmatic nature

Pace the rate or density of musical activities as perceived in relation to an established pattern of movement

Pan flute a type of aerophone comprised of individual tubes bound in raftlike form

Passion a vocal/choral work based on the biblical text related to the crucifixion of Christ

Penny whistle a simple type of aerophone popular in Ireland

Pentatonic scale a five-note scale with intervals reproducible on the black keys of the piano

Percussion a class of instruments that are normally struck

Phrase a more or less complex musical idea ending in a cadence

Pitch the musical equivalent of frequency

Plectrum (plural, plectra) a device for setting a string into motion; also known as a pick

Polyphony a texture consisting of two or more musical lines that vie for dominance

Prelude a composition title implying an introduction to a longer piece; also, a short, free-form piece

Pressure wave the periodic displacement of air that generates a sound

Pulse the marking of time in music

Rag an alternative spelling for raga

Rag a musical style developed in the United States that features highly syncopated melodies

Ragas scales and melodic figures that provide the basis for improvisation in Indian music

Recorder a type of aerophone

Register the relative highness or lowness of a voice or instrument

Resonance the acoustical enhancement of a sound

Resonator a device that aids the creation of resonance

Rhythm the organization of musical elements in time

Ritardando a slowing of tempo

Rondo a musical form that features the alternation of one section with contrasting sections, for example, *a b a c a b a*

Rubato   a momentary fluctuation of tempo

Shahnii   a type of double-reed aerophone from India

Shakuhachi   a type of aerophone from Japan; a Japanese flute

Shawm   a type of aerophone with a double reed

Sona   a type of double-reed aerophone from China

Sonata   an instrumental form generally several movements in length

Steel drums   Caribbean idiophones made from oil drums

Strings   a Euro-American class of instruments that includes violins, violas, cellos, and string basses

Subdominant chord   a chord built on the fourth step of the scale

Subsonic frequency   a sound too low to be perceived as pitch by the human ear

Suite   a set of pieces built on different dance rhythms

Surna   a type of double-reed aerophone from Turkey

Symphony   a large orchestral composition in three or four movements

Syncopation   the shifting of accent from a predictable beat

Tabla   a pair of tunable hand drums used in North Indian classical music

Tarka   a type of aerophone from the Andean region

Tempo   the relative speed of a piece as marked by the number of pulses within a given time span

Theme   a major musical idea in a complex musical form

Timbre   tone quality of a voice or instrument that is a result of the combination of harmonics

Toccata   most commonly an improvisational keyboard piece of a rhythmic nature

Tonic   the central or focal pitch of a tonal musical system

Tonic chord   a chord built on the first degree of the scale

Triad   a three-pitch chord

Trill   a rapid alternation between two pitches; used as an ornament

Ultrasonic frequency   a sound too high to be perceived as pitch by the human ear

Unison   more than one instrument or voice performing the same pitch, melody, or rhythm

Vibrato   a periodic alternation of a pitch to increase its expressive content

Vocal cords   parallel folds of tissue in the larynx—the source of sound in the human voice

Vocal mechanism   all of the parts of the human body involved in producing a vocal sound

Woodwinds   a Euro-American class of instruments that includes flutes, clarinets, oboes, bassoons, and saxophones

Zither   a type of chordophone with a series of fixed or movable bridges

REVIEW
TESTS

MUSICAL INVOLVEMENT: CHAPTER 1

Review Test

Q1   If the melody of short statements 1 and 2 generally moves from higher to lower pitches, what is the direction of long statement 1?

a. It also descends.

b. It generally rises.

c. It stays on the same general level.

d. It rises and descends.

Q2   Which sentence best describes short statements 1 and 2 and short statements 3 and 4?

a. 3 and 4 are exactly like 1 and 2.

b. 3 and 4 are totally different from 1 and 2

c. 1 and 3 are exactly alike but 3 and 4 are different

d. 3 and 4 are very similar to 1 and 2, but there is a change in instruments.

Q3.   Which statement (A, B, or C) is the shortest?

a. A

b. B

c. C

d. A and C

Q4   When do the drums enter?

a. The drums enter right away.

b. The drums come in and out.

c. The drums play at the very end.

d. The drums enter soon after the song begins.

Q5   After the flute enters, what is the nature of the accompaniment?

a. The lowest string instrument and the harpsichord are heard most prominently.

b. The entire orchestra plays all the time.

c. The harpsichord is heard alone.

d. The strings play without the harpsichord.

Q6   What happens to the mass of sound?

a. It remains constant throughout.

b. It decreases throughout.

c. It increases throughout.

d. It changes throughout with both increases and decreases.

Q7   How *might* these masses of sound be performed?

a. The masses cannot be played by the fingers and feet alone.

b. The masses can easily be played by the fingers.

225

Q8 How many pitches are the accompanying instruments playing?
   a. only one
   b. only two
Q9 Which statement best describes the sequence of entrances following the piano solo:
   a. The clarinet enters, followed by the oboe.
   b. The clarinet enters, followed by the flute.
   c. The flute enters, followed by the oboe.
   d. The oboe enters, followed by the clarinet.
Q10 How is the musical interest sustained throughout this example?
   a. The melody changes frequently.
   b. New rhythm patterns develop throughout.
   c. There are frequent changes in loudness.
   d. The listener's attention shifts from one conch shell to the other.
Q11 Two aerophones are also heard in this example. What are they?
   a. a flute and an oboe
   b. a trumpet and a trombone
   c. two conch shells
   d. two sirens
Q12 How are the violin strings set into vibration?
   a. only by plucking
   b. mostly by plucking and also bowed briefly
   c. only by bowing
   d. mostly by bowing but also plucked briefly
Q13 During which line in Part 1 does the chromelodeon return?
   a. line 1
   b. line 4
   c. line 5
   d. line 6
Q14 How many times is the phrase "Going home . . ." interjected in Part 1?
   a. five times
   b. eight times
   c. four times
   d. three times
Q15 Which two instruments are played most often during Part 2?
   a. diamond marimba and chromelodeon
   b. boo and diamond marimba
   c. chromelodeon and kithara
   d. kithara and boo

226

Q16 Which instrument is used only as a form of punctuation or emphasis in Part 2?
   a. chromelodeon
   b. kithara
   c. boo
   d. diamond marimba

Q17 How many instruments are used in Part 2?
   a. one
   b. two
   c. three
   d. four

MUSICAL INVOLVEMENT: CHAPTER 2

Review Test

Q1 Which singer is singing with the most physical exertion?
   a. the opera singer in Example 2.3
   b. the folksinger in Example 2.2

Q2 Which singer is closest to the microphone?
   a. the opera singer
   b. the folksinger

Q3 Which passage requires the greatest amount of energy?
   a. the first
   b. the second
   c. the third
   d. They are the same.

Q4 What is its relative speed?
   a. slow to moderate
   b. moderate to fast
   c. fast to very fast

Q5 What is it's relative range?
   a. very narrow
   b. moderate to wide
   c. very wide

Q6 How does the speed of vibrato compare with the singer in
   Example 2.3?
   a. The vibrato is slower.
   b. The vibrato is somewhat faster.
   c. The vibrato is much faster

Q7 Is vibrato used throughout the example or only at times?
   a. It is used sparingly.
   b. It is used only on important words.
   c. It is used throughout.

Q8 How is vibrato used?
   a. Very little vibrato is used.
   b. A great deal of vibrato is used.
   c. Certain words have a very distinctive vibrato.

Q9 What word in Line 1 features an elongated or stretched vowel
   sound?
   a. we
   b. ring
   c. children

Q10   The word *never* is heard four times in Lines 3 and 4. How many
      clearly pronounced final **r** sounds do you hear?
      a. one
      b. two
      c. three
Q11   During Line 7 one word is altered dramatically from normal
      speech rhythm. What is the word?
      a. were
      b. written
      c. stone
Q12   There is a somewhat long pause between two words in Line 8.
      The pause is between which of the following pairs of words?
      a. they/were
      b. were/true
      c. never/alone
Q13   The word *never* is heard twice during Line 8. Is the final **r** more
      audible on the first or the second *never?*
      a. the first
      b. the second
Q14   James Taylor is joined by other voices during two of the final
      four lines. Which two feature more than one voice?
      a. lines 9 and 10
      b. lines 9 and 11
      c. lines 10 and 11
      d. lines 10 and 12
Q15   During line 1, Vaughn uses vibrato on the word *rain* in two
      different ways. How do they differ?
      a. The first *rain* has vibrato thoughout; the second *rain* has no
         vibrato.
      b. The first has no vibrato; the second does.
      c. The first has a steady vibrato; the second begins with no
         vibrato but adds it later.
      d. The first begins with no vibrato and adds it; the second has
         continuous vibrato.
Q16   During line 2, what word is begun without vibrato but gradually
      adds it?
      a. before
      b. go
      c. something
      d. me

Q17 During line 4, there is glissando (slide) between two words. What are the words?
   a. it—isn't
   b. raining—rain
   c. it's—teardrops
Q18 What words in line 5 conclude with a short descending glissando?
   a. you/know
   b. sad/because
   c. heart/sings
   d. sad/heart
Q19 What word in line 6 receives a significant amount of ornamentation?
   a. bird
   b. fly
   c. broken
   d. wings
Q20 What word features a vowel exaggeration in line 8?
   a. why
   b. sky
   c. so
   d. gray
Q21 What word features a descending glissando in line 10?
   a. us
   b. cry
   c. it
   d. rained

NAME _____ INSTRUCTOR _____

COURSE NUMBER _____ SECTION _____ DATE _____

MUSICAL INVOLVEMENT: CHAPTER 3

Review Test

Q1 What instrument(s) create(s) a steady pulse?
   a. harpsichord
   b. recorders
   c. violins
   d. harpsichord and bass

Q2 How does the pace in the last section relate to the pace in the previous section?
   a. It is the same pace.
   b. It is a slower pace.
   c. It is a significantly faster pace.

Q3 Which of the four kinds of tempo change is used?
   a. an abrupt shift
   b. a gradual increase in basic pulse rate (accelerando)
   c. a gradual decrease in basic pulse rate (ritardando)
   d. a constant give-and-take in basic pulse rate (rubato)

Q4 Which of the four kinds of tempo change is used?
   a. an abrupt shift
   b. a gradual increase in basic pulse rate (accelerando)
   c. a gradual decrease in basic pulse rate (ritardando)
   d. a constant give-and-take in basic pulse rate (rubato)

Q5 What is the relationship between the two tempos of this example?
   a. One is pulsed and the other is not.
   b. The first is faster.
   c. The first is slower.

Q6 How does Berlioz change tempo from the first to the second section?
   a. with rubato
   b. with ritardando
   c. with an accelerando

Q7 Which of the four kinds of tempo change is used here?
   a. abrupt
   b. accelerando
   c. ritardando
   d. rubato throughout

Q8　How would you describe the two tempo changes?

　　a.　an abrupt shift followed by a rubato section

　　b.　an accelerando followed by a ritardando

　　c.　a ritardando followed by an abrupt return to the original tempo

　　d.　a ritardando followed by a rubato section

Q9　Most of the lines in the first part of this example demonstrate at least one type of tempo change. What line of the tenor solo (lines 1–9) has no tempo change?

　　a.　1

　　b.　3

　　c.　5

Q10　Which word in line 7 is subjected to the greatest change in tempo?

　　a.　Adunque

　　b.　Ah!

　　c.　donna

Q11　In lines 2 and 4 a single word (different in each line) is treated elaborately through ornamentation (the pace increases). What are the two words?

　　a.　del, qui,

　　b.　sua, umane

　　c.　core, sono

Q12　Which of the lines during the tenor solo has the greatest change of pace, that is, the largest number of syllables per pulse?

　　a.　line 8

　　b.　line 7

　　c.　line 6

Q13　Does the pace of the orchestral accompaniment increase or decrease from line 9 to 10 (at the beginning of the soprano passage)?

　　a.　It increases.

　　b.　It decreases.

Q14　Which line during the duet (lines 10–15) has the least ritardando?

　　a.　line 12

　　b.　line 13

　　c.　line 14

Q15　Is the pace at the beginning of line 12 faster or slower than in line 11?

　　a.　faster

　　b.　slower

Q16 In lines 10–15, during which line does the soprano move at a faster pace than the tenor?
   a. line 13
   b. line 14

MUSICAL INVOLVEMENT: CHAPTER 4

Review Test

Q1   At the basic level, are the pulses grouped by twos or threes?
 a. twos
 b. threes

Q2   At any level faster than the basic one are the pulses grouped by twos or threes?
 a. twos
 b. threes

Q3   Is there more than one pulse level heard in this example?
 a. no
 b. yes

Q4   Is the flute part syncopated?
 a. yes
 b. no

Q5   Are the main pulse groups of the bass twos or threes?
 a. twos
 b. threes

Q6   At the fast level of activity (mostly electric piano and snare drum), how many pulses are there to each main bass pulse?
 a. two
 b. three
 c. unequal groups of twos and three

Q7   Is the rate of rhythmic activity (pace) of the solo, faster, slower, or the same as the fast pulse rate of the beginning?
 a. slower
 b. faster
 c. same rate

Q8   Are there any sections of the solo itself that lack metrical definition?
 a. no
 b. yes, the high tones
 c. yes, the low tones
 d. yes, the long-held tones

Q9   At the outset, and several times thereafter, a new pulse rate comes into play. Does it quicken or slow the pace?
 a. It quickens the pace.
 b. It slows the pace

Q10 Does the bass continue with its original slow pulse group, or shift to a faster, syncopated figure?

a. It continues with the original slow pace.

b. It shifts to a faster syncopated figure.

Q11 Does the overall rate of rhythmic activity shift gradually or abruptly at the beginning of this section?

a. It doesn't change.

b. It shifts gradually.

c. It shifts abruptly.

Q12 Is the pulse rate of the violin solo generally the same as in the first section, or does it mostly coincide with the faster rate of other instruments?

a. It is the same.

b. It mostly coincide with the faster rate.

Q13 How many levels of two-pulse metric groups can you find between these extremes?

a. one

b. two

c. three

NAME ______________________ INSTRUCTOR ______________________

COURSE NUMBER __________ SECTION ______________ DATE __________

MUSICAL INVOLVEMENT: CHAPTER 5

Review Test

Q1 Which line in the diagram on the next page matches the full orchestral entrance after the brief piano introduction?
a. line 1
b. line 2
c. line 3

Q2 After the basic pattern is played by the full orchestra the clarinet has a solo, how does the rhythm of the clarinet part compare with the rhythm of the orchestral section?
a. It is identical.
b. It is very similar but not identical.
c. It is contrasting.

Q3 Which line in the following diagram matches the beginning of the first verse after the guitar introduction?
a. line 1
b. line 2
c. line 3

Q4 Is syncopation present in the excerpt?
a. yes
b. no

Q5 How does the rhythm of the second verse compare with that of the first?
a. It is an identical repetition.
b. It is a similar, but varied pattern.
c. It is a completely contrasting rhythm.

Q6 Which line in the following diagram matches the rhythm of the first statement?
a. line 1
b. line 2
c. line 3

Q7 How does the rhythm of the second statement compare with that of the first?
a. It is rhythmically identical.
b. It is the same, but with a difference at the beginning.
c. It is the same, but with a difference at the end.
d. It is different.

Q8 How does the rhythm of the third and fourth statements compare with that of the first and second statements?
a. It is in contrast.
b. It relates to the end of the first statement.
c. It relates to the beginning of the first statement.

Q9   Which line in the following diagram matches the first statement and response in the vocal line?
a. line 1
b. line 2
c. line 3

Q10 In the vocal line, is syncopation present in just the statement or in both statement and response?
a. in just the statement
b. in both statement and response

Q11 Is the second vocal statement and response rhythmically identical to or different from the first?
a. different from the first
b. identical to the first

Q12 In the vocal line, the pulse groups shift from twos to threes. Is the instrumental accompaniment consistently in twos or consistently in threes?
a. consistently in twos
b. consistently in threes

Q13 Which line in the diagram matches the fragment?
a. line 1
b. line 2
c. line 3

Q14 Considering the fragment in all its forms, how would you characterize its presence?
a. It is nearly always present.
b. It is absent for a considerable time.
c. It is presented for only the first half of the excerpt.
d. It is contrasted with a less memorable pattern that is used nearly as often.

Q15 Within the basic three pulse group is an implied pattern of short and long durations. Which pattern do you hear?
a. long—long—short
b. short—short—short
c. short—long—short

Q16 Which line in the diagram best matches the ostinato?
a. line 1
b. line 2
c. line 3

Q17 Where is the ostinato pattern in this historical dance rhythm (waltz) found?
a. in the melody
b. in the accompaniment

Q18 Where is the ostinato found?
    a. the vocal part
    b. the guitar
    c. the drums
    d. the bass guitar
Q19 Listen to the rhythm with the fastest pace. Does this ostinato move consistently and without interruption or is it syncopated?
    a. consistently and without interruption
    b. syncopated
Q20 How many ostinatos are heard?
    a. one
    b. two
    c. three
Q21 Which words accompany this pattern:
    a. When I am laid in earth
    b. May my wrongs create
    c. But ah! forget my fate
    d. When I am laid, am laid in earth
Q22 A bit later, the following pattern emerges (with silences in the vocal line indicated by the blank spots in the diagram). What are the accompanying words?
    a. My wrongs create
    b. Remember me, remember me
    c. Remember me, but ah!
    d. Forget my fate, forget my fate
Q23 As the air begins, the orchestra commences an ostinato in the bass which has the following pitch contour and rhythm. How many times does this ostinato occur?
    a. twice
    b. six
    c. eleven

MUSICAL INVOLVEMENT: CHAPTER 6

Review Test

Q1 How do the tonic pitches relate to the accented beats?
    a. They never fall on accented beats.
    b. They always fall on accented beats.
    c. They fall on accented on unaccented beats an equal number of times.
    d. They fall accented beats most of the time.

Q2 Does section two end on a tonic or non-tonic pitch?
    a. tonic
    b. non-tonic

Q3 The pitches on the three words in question are:
    a. tonic on the first two and non-tonic on the last
    b. tonic on all three
    c. tonic on the last word only
    d. tonic on the first two only

Q4 How many pitches are used?
    a. one
    b. two
    c. three
    d. four

Q5 Are the two instruments playing different pitch successions (melodies), or are they simply playing two versions of the same melody, one more elaborate than the other?
    a. two different melodies
    b. the exact same melody
    c. two different versions

Q6 Where does the change from minor to major occur?
    a. during line 2
    b. during line 3
    c. during line 4
    d. during line 5

Q7 Where does the change back to minor occur?
    a. during line 3
    b. during line 4
    c. during line 5
    d. during line 6

Q8　On what words do the changes take place in the second verse?
　　a. "town"/"brown"
　　b. "street"/"feet"
　　c. "star"/"head"

Q9　Does the pattern continue in the same way or does it change?
　　a. It remains the same.
　　b. It changes

Q10　On what words of the text in verses 1 and 2 does this chord change take place?
　　a. "there'll be"/"gonna be"
　　b. "gonna be"/"rock'n"
　　c. "mama"/"there'll be"

Following are lines from three songs. On what words do the chords change? (more than one answer may be correct)

Q11　Mary had a little lamb, little lamb, little lamb
　　a. first "little lamb"
　　b. second "little lamb"
　　c. third "little lamb"

Q12　Silent night, holy night, all is calm, all is bright
　　a. "silent night"/"all is calm"
　　b. "holy night"/"all is bright"
　　c. "all is calm"/"all is bright"

Q13　Old MacDonald had a farm, ee-i-ee-i-o
　　a. "MacDonald's"
　　b. "farm"
　　c. "a"
　　d. "ee-i-ee-i-o"

Q14　Does the chord succession change or stay the same during the instrumental sections?
　　a. It changes.
　　b. It remains the same.

Q15　Compare the relative importance of Ga & Ni in the following example.
　　a. Ga is more important in this example.
　　b. Ni is more important.
　　c. They are of equal importance.

Q16　Which subsection contains the gesture N R S?
　　a. section a
　　b. section d
　　c. section e
　　d. section g

244

Q17 How would you describe the relationship between 6:14a and 6:14b?
 a. There is no pattern of variation.
 b. The pattern is created by first playing the next pitch of the nuclear theme twice and then playing the principal pitch twice.
 c. The pattern is created by first playing the principal pitch twice and then playing the next pitch of the nuclear theme twice.
 d. A combination of B and C.
Q18 How does the pattern of silences develop?
 a. There is no pattern.
 b. After an irregular pattern there is an alternation (at principal pitches) of a unison pitch and a silence.
 c. The pattern is regular.
Q19 What is the pattern of elaboration?
 a. The elaboration is always based on the principal pitch and the next pitch in the nuclear theme.
 b. The elaboration is always based on the principal pitch and two pitches forward.
 c. The elaboration is based on the principal pitch and the previous pitch.
 d. The elaboration is based on the principal pitch and/or the next or next two pitches of the nuclear theme.

MUSICAL INVOLVEMENT: CHAPTER 8

Review Test

Q1   Is the Bach pulsed or nonpulsed?
  a. pulsed
  b. nonpulsed

Q2   Subsection A, Subsection B, and Subsection A^1 are made up of pairs of phrases. In which subsection are the two phrases alike in all regards?
  a. Subsection A
  b. Subsection B
  c. Subsection A^1

Q3   In which phrase does the instrument playing the primary melody change?
  a. phrase 1
  b. phrase 3
  c. phrase 5
  d. phrase 7

Q4   What is the major difference between phrases 7 and 8?
  a. The melody is totally different.
  b. The melody in phrase 8 is the same but the length of each pitch is doubled.
  c. The melody in phrase 8 is the same but each pitch is played more quickly.

Q5   Do they grow out of motives, or are they primarily phrase generated?
  a. They grow out of motives.
  b. They are primarily phrase generated.

Q6   Are phrases equal or unequal in length in the first group? in the second group?
  a. They are equal in both groups.
  b. They are equal in the first group, unequal in the second.
  c. They are unequal in the first group, equal in the second.
  d. They are unequal in both groups.

Q7   Which group generates the most tension? (Hint: what was your answer to Q6?)
  a. the first group
  b. the second group

Q8 Consider and compare the pitch level and rhythmic patterns of the foreground instruments and the role of the background instruments in Sections 1 and 2. Which statement best describes their relationship?
a. All of the elements stay the same.
b. All of the elements change during Section 2.
c. The background remains the same in both sections and the foreground changes both in pitch level and rhythmic patterns in Section 2.

Q9 Which is the principal means of variation in phrase 2 of Section 1: change of pitch level or change of rhythmic pattern?
a. change of pitch level
b. change of rhythmic pattern

Q10 In Section 2 are phrases 1 and 2 more or less elaborate melodically than they are in Section 1?
a They are much more elaborate.
b. They are slightly more elaborate.
c. They stay the same.

Q11 Is the greatest contrast at the beginning or at the end of phrase 3? How is this contrast created?
a. at the beginning, by a higher pitch level and more complex rhythm
b. at the end, by a more active accompaniment

Q12 Does phrase 4 differ from 1 and 2 mostly in pitch or in rhythm?
a. mostly in pitch
b. mostly in rhythm

Q13 The introduction, interludes between the second and third verses, and conclusion are played on the dulcimer. Are the interludes the same length as the introduction?
a. Yes, they are the same.
b. No, they are shorter.
c. No, they are longer.

Q14 In verse 1, what are the words that coincide on the elisions?
a. God and said, good and brother
b. light and God; night and God; day and day

Q15 Where does the cadence occur?
a. near the beginning
b. near the middle
c. near the end

Q16 Is the musical material of (3) different from or the same as (1)?
a. different
b. the same

Q17 Are the transitions more closely related to the quality of rhythmic movement in section (1) or section (3)?
a. They are more closely related to section (1).
b. They are more closely related to section (3).

Q18 The term "presentation" suggest greater musical significance than "continuation-transition," but there is an element in (2) that contradicts this assumption. What is the element?
a. The continuation-transition is much shorter than the presentation.
b. The continuation-transition is much longer than the presentation.
c. The continuation-transition consists of new motivic material.

Q19 Which element in section (3) gives it the open-ended and forward-moving quality?
a. a recitative-like quality in the accompaniment
b. more complex rhythmic variety
c. many ascending melodic phrases
d. all of the above

Q20 How is section (4) different from section (1)?
a. It is played at a faster pace.
b. The solo violin is not playing.
c. It is played at a different pitch level.
d. all of the above

Q21 Which pair of motives appears first—3 and 5 or 1 and 2?
a. 3 and 5
b. 1 and 2

Q22 Two motives appear next in quick succession; are they 3 and 4 or 4 and 5?
a. 3 and 4
b. 4 and 5

Q23 Which motive is used more often throughout—3 or 4?
a. 3
b. 4

Q24 Which motive is present almost constantly—2 or 5?
a. 2
b. 5

Q25 Which motives are brought together tightly to produce a climax at the end?
   a. 1, 3, and 5
   b. 3, 4 and 5
   c. 1, 2 and 5

Q26 In general, what happens to the register as the piece nears its conclusion?
   a. It moves higher.
   b. It moves lower.
   c. It stays the same.

MUSICAL INVOLVEMENT: CHAPTER 9
Review Test

Q1 Which factors contribute to the continuity of this piece?
   a. even pulse; unison passages
   b. use of organ and keyboard percussion throughout
   c. sustained sounds; whispers; vocal outbursts

Q2 Which factors contribute to the continuity of this piece?
   a. tempo and balance
   b. ostinato and variation
   c. motivic and tonal relationships

Q3 How does Handel reflect the power of the word "healed"?
   a. He states it only in a solo voice.
   b. He quickens the pace each time the word is sung.
   c. The word has the longest time value in the phrase.
   d. He eliminates the instrumental accompaniment during the word.

Q4 Compare the first and the second refrains.
   a. They are exactly the same.
   b. They are slightly varied.
   c. They are extremely varied.

Q5 In what way is the final refrain different from all the others?
   a. It is twice as long.
   b. It is sung at a faster pace.
   c. It changes to the major tonality; all the other refrains are in minor.

Q6 What does the performer do to provide some variety in the repeated statements within Section A at the beginning and end?
   a. The performer changes the color of the harpsichord's sound.
   b. The performer varies the tempo with rubato.
   c. The performer pauses between the repeated statements.

Q7 In general, one expects the recurrence of a musical idea following a contrasting section to lower tension by returning to familiar ground, but in this case tension increases when A^1 begins. Why?
   a. A^1 is an instrumental section.
   b. Instead of returning to the initial melody, the singer varies it greatly, starting at a higher pitch level.
   c. Instead of returning to the initial melody, the singer varies it greatly, starting at a lower pitch level.
   d. The singer changes the words when A^1 begins.

Q8   During the exposition, how does the transition function?
    a. It glides smoothly from *a* to *b* without a break.
    b. It interrupts for a new idea.
    c. It interrupts for a further treatment of *a*.

Q9   Compare the musical character of *a* and *b* ?
    a. b is less aggressive.
    b. b is more aggressive.
    c. b is initially more gentle and then more aggressive.

Q10   How does the close of the exposition relate to the earlier material?
    a. It is closely related to *b*.
    b. It is entirely new.
    c. It is closely related to *a*.

Q11   How does the material treated in the development relate to the material in the exposition?
    a. It is derived solely from *a*.
    b. It is derived solely from *b*.
    c. It is related to both *a* and *b*.
    d. It is unrelated to either *a* or *b*.

Q12   What is the primary role of the piano?
    a. It plays a rhythmic accompaniment.
    b. It plays block chords.
    c. It plays a bass line.
    d. It plays an ornamental melody.

Q13   What is the role of the bass in this section?
    a. It plays an independent melody.
    b. It plays part of the background chords.
    c. It plays a variation of the theme.
    d. It is not playing in this section.

Q14   During Variation 3, what is the role of the violin and viola?
    a. They play a rhythmic accompaniment.
    b. They play the melody.
    c. They play sustained chords
    d. They do not play in this section.

Q15   During Variation 4, what is the role of the bass?
    a. It is active on nearly every pulse.
    b. It sustains long notes.
    c. It is melodic.

Q16   Which two instruments share the theme?
    a. violin and viola
    b. violin and piano
    c. violin and cello
    d. violin and bass

Q17 Which two instruments exchange the darting figure?
   a. violin and viola
   b. violin and piano
   c. violin and cello
   d. violin and bass
Q18 Which scheme represents the missing small letters in the B section?
   a. a^1–a
   b. b^1–b
   c. a–b
   d. c–b
Q19 In which variation of A do you hear singular interjections of high register pitches?
   a. A^1
   b. A^2
   c. A^3
Q20 Which of the following statements best reflects the relationship between musical structures and tension/repose?
   a. Repeated recurrences of a theme heighten tension.
   b. Repeated recurrences of a theme heighten repose.
   c. The recurrence of a theme after new material is introduced provides tension.
   d. The recurrence of a theme after new material is introduced provides repose.

MUSICAL INVOLVEMENT: CHAPTER 10

Review Test

Q1 Does the concluding vocal passage further relax the tension or raise it to a new level?
   a. It relaxes the tension.
   b. It does not change the tension level.
   c. It raises the tension to a new level.

Q2 Is the phrase that follows this recurrence again long and unbalanced or is it the same length as the opening phrase?
   a. It is long and unbalanced.
   b. It is the same length as the opening phrase.

Q3 Is this phrase longer or shorter than the ten-group phrase?
   a. It is longer—twice as long, in fact.
   b. It is the same length.
   c. It is shorter.

Q4 What effect does the length of this phrase have on tension?
   a. It increases tension.
   b. It has a calming effect because of its length.
   c. It has no effect on the level of tension.

Q5 The two-part phrase described above is immediately repeated. Does this raise or lower tension? Why?
   a. It raises tension, because the repetition pushes the listener past the point of tolerance.
   b. It raises tension because the listener expects variation.
   c. It lowers tension because of the repose of repetition.

Q6 After this repetition, a contrasting two-part phrase is introduced. The second part of this new phrase is a slightly varied repetition of the first part. What tension-repose effects are provided by the slight variation?
   a. The variation raises tension.
   b. The variation lowers tension.
   c. The variation has no effect on the tension level.

Q7 Which version has more new information, and therefore more tension, in the repetition of the first phrase?
   a. the Mozart
   b. the Dohnányi

Q8 What elements in the Dohnányi provide the tension-creating surprises?
   a. the gradual quickening of the pace and the use of the trombone
   b. the use of rubato, changing harmony and bassoon
   c. the sudden dynamic changes and the use of the harpsichord

259

Q9　Like most listeners, you very likely expect phrase a to be answered by a phrase of equal length. How does Mozart raise the tension by denying your expectations?

　　a. He makes the answering phrase (a^1) half again as long.

　　b. He makes the answering phrase (a^1) twice as long.

　　c. He makes the answering phrase (a^1) twice as short.

Q10　Phrases a^2 and a^3 are related to a and a^1. What elements of a^3 raise the tension further?

　　a. a^3 is slower and softer.

　　b. a^3 begins in a different tonality than a^2.

　　c. a^3 is longer still than a^1 and more complex in density.

Q11　Phrases a^5 and a^6 are a recurrence of a and a^1, with the same length relationship. What changes prevent them from providing the repose of an exact recurrence?

　　a. The register is changed.

　　b. The register is changed and played by a single instrument.

　　c. The register is changed and the tonality shifts.

　　d. The register is changed and more material is added to accompany the melody.

Q12　What expectation aroused by a and denied by a^1 is finally fulfilled by a^7 and a^8?

　　a. a^8 returns to the tonic pitch.

　　b. a^7 and a^8 are equal in length.

　　c. a^8 is an exact repetition of a.

Q13　Which phrase reaches the highest level of tension because of the complexity of its contents—the number of things to take in simultaneously?

　　a. a^1

　　b. a^4

　　c. a^6

　　d. a^8

Q14　Why does the sustained sound in Section 1 create tension?

　　a. It is a variation of the opening.

　　b. It gets softer just as you expect it to get louder.

　　c. It comes as a surprise, its instrumentation is different, and its pitch doesn't "fit" the pitch relationships of the passage as a whole.

Q15　What factors contribute to rising tension in Section 2?

　　a. gradual increase in loudness; length and increased activity

　　b. sameness of instrumentation and volume

　　c. the overload of musical information

Q16   Does Section 3 provide more or less tension than Section 2?
      a. More, because it is faster.
      b. More, because the density is greater.
      c. Less, because of the tranquility of the melody.
      d. Less, because its simplicity relieves the nervous energy built
         up in Section 2.
Q17   Does Section 4 create repose, tension, or both, in relation to what
      has gone before?
      a. Repose, because it is a return of the kind of activity of Section
         2.
      b. Tension, because of the variation of the added instruments.
      c. Repose, through return to the kind of activity of Section 2;
         tension through added instruments.
Q18   Sections 3 and 5 begin similarly. Which reaches a higher level of
      tension?
      a. Section 3, because it is the first time we have heard this
         material.
      b. Section 5, through an unexpected extension in relation to
         Section 3.
      c. Section 5, because it is much shorter and more dense than
         Section 3.
Q19   Does Section 6 bring more repose or greater tension?
      a. More repose, because of its comparative simplicity.
      b. More repose, because the brass instruments do not play.
      c. Greater tension, because of the fast-moving melody.
      d. Greater tension, because we are expecting a return of an
         earlier passage.
Q20   Which set of musical elements could be described as tension-
      decreasers in this example?
      a. the surprise of silence and uncertainty about its length;
         sudden loud, sustained tone; onset of flutter-tonguing
      b. unexpected silences; repetition of similar sounds; homogene-
         ity of brass tones
      c. repetition of similar sounds; soft, sustained passage; quiet
         conclusion
Q21   Which version strikes you as the simpler, more straightforward
      presentation of the tune?
      a. Example 10.12
      b. Example 10.13
Q22   What overall factors in 10.13 create a level of tension somewhat
      higher than the level in 10.12?
      a. a higher pitched tonal center; larger group
      b. a much longer introduction; unstable pulse groupings
      c. more rhythmic energy, more variation

261

Q23 In which version does the introduction have a greater measure of tension? Why?

    a. Example 10.12. There is no sense of how long it will last and where the melody will begin.

    b. Example 10.13. The piano part is more complex, and the drums add momentum.

Q24 Compare phrase a in the two versions. What surprise raises the tension in 10.13?

    a. The melody suddenly drops out.

    b. The piano takes over the melodic line.

    c. The rhythm stops.

    d. The trumpet improvises on the melody.

Q25 Why do phrases b and a^2 of 10.13 have a higher tension level than the same phrases in 10.12?

    a. The listener is expecting an exact recurrence.

    b. The meter shifts in the accompaniment.

    c. The trumpet sound is uniquely different.

    d. There is more variation, together with a higher pitch level, and more unexpected pitches.

INDEX

Page numbers in *italic* indicate illustrations.
Composers or origins of music appear in boldface.

Syncopation, 79, 86–87
Synthesizer, 40, 109–10

Tabor, *23*
Tamboura, 84, 132
Tarka, 16
Tartini: *Symphony in A Major,* 3rd
    mvt., 78
Taylor: *Never Die Young,* 58
Tchaikovsky:
    1812 Overture, 145
    Swan Lake, "Valse," 86, 105
Tempo, 69–73
    changes in, 70–73
    defined, 70
Tension
    in four-phrase section, 172
    return to tonic and, 117
    in rondo form, 188, 190
Tension and repose, 203–18
    in chord progressions, 124–27
    expectation and surprise in,
        206–7
    levels of, 203–5
    metrical conflict and ambiguity
        in, 86
    pace and, 67
    repetition and, 209–12
    return to tonic and, 124
    rhythmic patterns and, 94, 95
    sources of, 205–18
    superimposed meter and, 87–88
    suppressed meter and, 89
    syncopation and, 79
    tempo and, 73
Ternary design, 188–90, 200
That, 128–30
Theremin, 40
Thirds, 122–23
Time frame, 65–75
    pace and, 67–69
    tempo and, 69–73

B 2
C 3
D 4
E 5
F 6
G 7
H 8
I 9
J 0

Tonality, 111–14
Tonic, 115
    defined, 111
    in chords, 124–27
Transitional passages, 175–77
Transposing of keys, 119
Triads, 123
Trombone, 27
Trumpet, 26, 27
Trumpet-type instruments, 26–29
Tuba, 27
Twinkle, Twinkle, Little Star,
    93–94
Two-partness, 197–98

Varèse: *Ionisation,* 33
Variation
    in conventional structure,
        193–96
    in mixed structure, 200
    rhythmic, 95
Velez: *Blue Castle,* 82
Verdi: *Rigoletto,* "Love Is the
    Flame," 74
Vibrato, 50–53
Violin, *34, 35*
Voice
    diction and, 54–59
    expressive devices of, 50–53
    genetics and conditioning in,
        47–48
    as instrument, 45–63
    power of, 48–50

Waltz, 152
Winter: *Rock and Roll,* 124
Woodwinds, 12–26

Xenakis: *Akrata,* 213
Xylophone, 135–36

Yaman, 130–33

Zheng, 36
Zither, 36